from Brenn
Sept 20

Artichoke Extravaganza

"HUZZAH! Long Live the Artichoke!"
From its inception until this past year, Manny was the extravagant
proprietor of the artichoke booth and the original California Renaissance
Pleasure Faire. The artichoke booth was an integral part of Faire legend.
Many people fondly remember eating the huge thistles, drenched in
herb butter, while sitting on hay bales, watching the Commedia
dell'arte, the jugglers, or the arrival of Gloriana herself and thrilling to
the shouts of "Huzzah! Huzzah! Long Live the Queen!" It is to the
memory of Manny and grand memories of the Faire that this book is
most fondly dedicated.

Rio Nuevo Publishers®
P.O. Box 5250, Tucson, Arizona 85703-0250
(520) 623-9558, www.rionuevo.com

Text and photography copyright © 2009 by Rio Nuevo Publishers.

Food styling by Amy Edelen.
Recipe on pages 56–57 by Chef Colin Moody, CCC.

Photography/Illustration credits as follows:
Scott Calhoun: photos on front cover; pages 3, 11, 49
W. Ross Humphreys: photos on back cover; pages 4 right, 5, 8, 9,
10, 12, 13, 14, 28, 33, 44, 57, 71, 81
Robin Stancliff: photos on pages 4 left, 16, 17, 19, 23, 34, 40, 63, 66

Library of Congress Cataloging-in-Publication Data

Duncann, Geraldine.
Artichoke extravaganza / Geraldine Duncann.
    p. cm. -- (Cook West series)
Includes index.
ISBN-13: 978-1-933855-20-2 (pbk. : alk. paper)
ISBN-10: 1-933855-20-7 (pbk. : alk. paper) 1. Cookery (Artichokes)
I. Title.
TX803.A7D96 3009
641.3'532--dc22

                                    2009016874

Design: Karen Schober, Seattle, Washington

Printed in Korea.

10 9 8 7 6 5 4 3 2 1

artichoke

extravaganza

GERALDINE DUNCANN

COOK WEST
SERIES

RIO NUEVO PUBLISHERS
TUCSON, ARIZONA

contents

AN AEGEAN LEGEND

It was a golden day as the lovely maiden was playing on the shore of the Aegean Sea, dancing in and out of the waves and cavorting with the dolphins and sea horses. Zeus, who had been visiting his brother Poseidon, spied her as he emerged from the sea. He was so smitten by her beauty that he could not control his desire and so, exerting his *droit du seigneur,* he seduced her on the spot. She so pleased him that he elevated her to the status of a goddess and took her back to Olympus with him. At first the girl greatly enjoyed the attention and her new status; however, after a while she became homesick for her mother and her mortal lover and took to slipping back to earth whenever Zeus was away. When Zeus discovered her betrayal he was so outraged that he hurled her back to earth and transformed her into an artichoke plant, thinking that her rough and thistly appearance would keep all others from being attracted to her.

Well, the last laugh was on Zeus, because ever since, people have been attracted to the artichoke.

So, who wants to eat a thistle? Anyone with discriminating **A BIT OF HISTORY**
taste buds, that's who! After all, an artichoke is just a thistle
that got carried away with its own importance, and people
have been eating thistles for over 2,000 years.

This member of the sunflower family, which originally grew
wild throughout the Mediterranean, is generally thought to
have first been cultivated in Sicily; however, there are botanists
and food historians who believe its cultivation may have first
occurred on the Italian mainland or in Greece.

Written records as well as images on frescoes and mosaics
and even petrified remains of table scraps found in Pompeii
indicate that the early cultivated varieties were very similar to
the beautiful globe artichokes we enjoy today.

Artichokes became such a popular item in the Roman diet that
most home gardens included them. There were even printed
instructions describing how to propagate them from both seeds
and cuttings. As popular as the artichoke was, it was not widely
cultivated for commercial production until around the eighth cen-

tury A.D., and even then remained mainly in the Mediterranean. Artichokes did not start making much of a show in northern Europe until around the twelfth century, and even then they were not very popular. It wasn't until Catherine de Médicis arrived from Florence in 1533 to marry the Duke d'Orléans, who later became Henry II of France, that the artichoke became a popular part of the French diet. She is credited with having introduced many favorite Italian dishes to the French cuisine.

Artichokes enjoyed a brief bit of popularity in Elizabethan England and then lapsed into virtual obscurity in the English diet. Even today it is a rare item, seldom seen in markets, and making only rare appearances in upscale restaurants.

There are records indicating that artichokes were a part of the Native American diet, but those were Jerusalem artichokes, a root, and not the thistle that is more commonly known today. The first actual artichoke plants were imported into the New World in the sixteenth century when Franciscan *padres* planted them in the gardens of the missions they established along the coast of California. At Mission La Purísima Concepción, which is now a state park, there are artichokes growing in the restored gardens that are reputed to be descendents of the originals planted by the founding padres. French settlers also brought the starts for artichokes to Louisiana, but the artichoke never became a viable commercial crop there.

As a fifth-generation Californian, I am proud to state that we enjoy the distinction of producing nearly 100 percent of the U.S. commercial artichoke crop. Over 80 percent of that comes from a small area around Castroville in Monterey County, south of San Francisco. However, the artichoke didn't really take off as a commercial crop in California until the 1920s. The Castroville region boasts a unique climate, perfect for the cultivation of artichokes. Due to its close proximity to the sea, the temperature is relatively stable year-round, seldom freezing and never reaching the high summer temperatures of the inland valleys. Even in mid-summer, the cooling sea mists roll in every day and moderate the temperature. This makes for very happy artichokes.

The world's largest producer of artichokes is Italy, with Spain running a close second. There are about 140 classified varieties of artichoke plants, but only four varieties are grown commercially in the U.S. About thirty varieties are grown in Italy. If you've ever driven through Castroville and marveled at field after field of artichokes stretching out to the horizon, consider this: Italy produces over one billion pounds of artichokes each year, and nearly all are eaten locally!

THE PLANT

Artichoke plants can get as large as four to six feet in height and diameter. The plants send up several long shoots, each producing several large artichokes. What are known as baby artichokes grow on low side shoots, or sucker stems, which come directly from the ground below the leaves of the plant. These will never mature into large plants and are sold canned or fresh as baby artichokes or artichoke hearts.

Artichokes are now available throughout the year, though they reach their peak in spring and autumn.

Spring artichokes tend to be compact, firm, and heavy for their size. Baby artichokes are also plentiful in the spring. Summer artichokes tend to have longer thorns, and their leaves are more open in appearance. Winter artichokes are often a bit more conical in shape. Some fall and winter artichokes may be "winter kissed," touched by frost. When this happens they may turn a light bronze in color. Winter-kissed artichokes tend to have a nutty, rich flavor, not present the rest of the year.

FASCINATING FACTS

- The name "artichoke" is thought to come from the Arabic *alqarchuf*.
- The ancient Romans candied baby artichokes in honey, lemon, and crushed cumin seed. They considered the artichoke an aphrodisiac, finding its shape erotic.
- Marilyn Monroe was crowned the first queen of the Castroville Artichoke Festival in 1947. The festival is held each year in the spring and features many activities, including a parade, the crowning of the Artichoke Queen, music, and numerous food booths selling artichokes. For information visit: www.artichoke-festival.org.
- Ancient Greeks thought that if their wives ate artichokes it would guarantee that they would give birth to sons.
- In a cookbook owned by Martha Washington there is a recipe entitled "To Make Hartichoke Pie."
- The poet Johann Wolfgang von Goethe (1749–1832) in his *Travels through Italy,* wrote, "The peasants eat thistles. A practice I can never adopt."
- In 1922, Andrew Molera, a landowner in the Salinas Valley of Monterey County, California, just south of San Francisco, decided to lease his land, which was previously used to grow sugar beets, to Italian farmers. He encouraged them to grow the "new" vegetable, artichokes. In a few years his revenue from the land tripled.

DIET AND HEALTH   As early as the fourth century B.C., Theophrastus, a pupil of Aristotle, claimed that the artichoke was effective in the treatment of various diseases of the liver and the blood.

Today, over two thousand years later, both holistic and white-coat practitioners are discovering that an extract from the leaves, buds, and flowers of the globe artichoke is useful in the treatment of gallbladder and liver aliments, as well as anemia, diabetes, kidney disease, and high cholesterol.

Fresh artichokes are low in calories and sodium, are fat- and cholesterol-free, and are a good source of fiber and vitamins A, B, and C.

The following nutritional facts are for one (10-ounce) steamed or boiled artichoke:

Calories: 60	Total carbohydrates: 13.4g
Calories from fat: 1	Dietary fiber: 6.5g
Total fat: 0.2g	Protein: 4.2g
Saturated fat: 0g	Vitamin A: 212mg
Polyunsaturated fat: 0.1g	Vitamin B_6: 0.1mg
Monounsaturated fat: 0g	Vitamin C: 12mg
Cholesterol: 0g	Calcium: 54mg
Sodium: 397mg	Magnesium: 72mg
Potassium: 424mg	Iron: 1mg

THE BASICS

Choosing a Good 'Choke   Always choose artichokes that are heavy for their size and have tightly closed leaves. Their color should be olive-green or lightly touched with bronze. The leaves should not feel papery.

Basic Cooking   This is where I greatly disagree with most cooks. I do not chop off and discard the greater part of the artichoke. I utilize as much of it as possible.

First, cut the stem off flush with the bottom of the artichoke so that it can sit flat, but don't discard the stem. Cook it along

with the artichoke. If the artichoke was young the stem may be tender for an inch or two and will taste like the heart. Pull off the tiny, superficial leaves that are growing around the bottom of the artichoke.

Next, with a sharp knife, trim off only about the top ½–1 inch of the artichoke. Then take a pair of kitchen scissors and snip off the very tip of each leaf. This will remove the tiny stickers. Now you may boil or steam the artichokes until they are tender. They are done when you can easily pull off one of the leaves. Remove them from the pot, turn upside down, and allow to completely drain. Some cooks like to put a bit of olive oil in the boiling water. I do not, simply to avoid the extra calories. It makes them nice but it certainly isn't necessary.

This is the basic way to cook and serve an artichoke. Each person pulls off the leaves and eats them plain or enhances them with a sauce of choice: melted butter, mayonnaise, aioli, hollandaise, etc. To eat the leaves, put the fleshy end in your mouth

TIPS

- Never throw away the leaves when a dish calls for the hearts only. Save them and serve with mayonnaise or another dip as a healthful snack.
- Don't discard the stems. Cook them with the artichoke, and taste them to see if they are tender.
- Fresh-cooked and chilled artichokes are easy to keep on hand for quick meals. Refrigerated in a covered container, they will keep for up to a week.
- Wherever a recipe calls for canned broth, the equivalent in homemade broth may be used. A 15½-ounce can equals about 2 cups; a 49½-ounce can equals about 6 cups.

and pull it through your teeth, which removes the soft part of the leaf. Discard the remaining leaf. When you have eaten all the leaves you may then scrape out the thistle (see "Removing the Choke," below) and enjoy the delectable bonus, the heart.

This basic cooking method is also the starting point for many of the recipes you will find in this book.

Removing the Choke   To remove the choke from the center of a cooked artichoke, pull out the center tuft of leaves with your fingers and discard. Spread the remaining leaves out a bit, and with a spoon carefully scrape out the thistly part, leaving the heart. Your artichoke is now ready to serve in a variety of ways. It may be stuffed or used as a bowl for serving dips and such.

Since fine, fresh California artichokes are not always readily available in all regions of the country, many of the recipes in this book utilize canned or frozen artichokes. These products are packaged either as baby artichokes or artichoke hearts. They are the very small artichokes that grow at the bottom of the plant.

They most commonly come in 6-ounce jars in a marinade, in 14-ounce cans packed in water, or frozen in 8-ounce bags (about 1½ cups). The marinated ones have their place in salads and other applications where the permeating flavor of the marinade is appropriate. The canned water-pack and frozen varieties have a wider application since they are not pre-seasoned. Canned water-pack and frozen artichokes are mostly interchangeable.

And so, it is my hope that this collection of recipes will help you bring a bit of California sunshine to your table, no matter where you live.

Enjoy!

Artichoke Marilyn (The Golden Artichoke)

xxxxxx

I created this delectable dish to honor Marilyn Monroe, a delectable lady, who was crowned the first Artichoke Queen of the Castroville Artichoke Festival in 1947. Although it makes an excellent party munchie, it also makes for an elegant and romantic dinner for two. Try feeding it to each other in front of a fire, accompanied by Champagne, of course.

Serves 2 as an entrée, or 4 as an appetizer

1 very large artichoke

½ cup grated extra sharp Cheddar

½ cup grated high-quality Swiss cheese such as Emmenthaler or Gruyère

2 tablespoons cornstarch

About ¼ pound cooked baby shrimp meat, flaked cooked crabmeat, or a combination

½ cup finely chopped yellow onion

1 green onion, finely chopped, including most of the green

1 tablespoon each finely minced fresh dill weed, basil, and cilantro

2 cloves garlic, very finely minced

½ cup fresh salsa, medium

3 eggs, lightly beaten

2 tablespoons sweet and hot brown mustard (page 86) or commercial

½ cup slivered, toasted almonds *

Salt and freshly coarse-ground black pepper

Trim and cook the artichoke (page 11). Boil the trimmed-off stem along with the artichoke. Cook until you can just pull off a leaf, but not until the artichoke is falling apart. Remove from the pot, set upside down, and allow to drain and cool thoroughly. Preheat the oven to 350 degrees F. Meanwhile, toss the cheeses with the cornstarch and set aside. Chop the shrimp or crab small and put into a medium mixing bowl. Add the next seven ingredients and mix well. If the stem of the artichoke is tender, chop it very small and add to the mixture. With a rolling pin, crush the almonds and add. Season to taste with salt and pepper. Mix well.

Remove the choke when the artichoke is completely cooled (page 13). Set the artichoke in an ovenproof serving bowl. You will most likely have to use your hands for the next step. Fill the center of the artichoke with the cheese/seafood mixture. Then, gently shove some of it down among the leaves until there is a bit of the filling between each leaf. Put in the preheated oven and bake for about 30 minutes or until the filling is set. Remove from the oven and allow to cool for a few minutes before serving. Each diner pulls off a leaf, which will have a bit of the filling stuck to it. Be sure to provide napkins and a receptacle for the used leaves. When the leaves are eaten you can fight over who gets the heart. Nice guys share.

* You want the type of almonds that are in thin slices, not the ones that are little spears.

Artichokes with Three Dips
xxxxxx

Serves 8–12 as an appetizer

In this tasty recipe, each artichoke doubles as a serving dish for its own dipping sauce.

3 large artichokes

Sprigs of fresh dill weed and/or basil, for garnish

Lemon wedges, for garnish

Trim, cook, and drain the artichokes (page 11). When the artichokes are cool enough to handle, remove the chokes (page 13). Refrigerate until ready to serve.

Alternate serving methods shown.

CLAM DIP

Mix all ingredients together and refrigerate until ready to serve. *Makes about 1½ cups*

1 cup sour cream

1 can (6½ ounces) minced clams, drained (juice reserved)

¼ cup reserved clam juice

1 tablespoon very finely minced green onion

1 clove garlic, very finely minced

1 tablespoon finely minced fresh dill weed

1 teaspoon Worcestershire sauce

Juice of ½ lemon, or to taste

Tabasco sauce

Salt and freshly coarse-ground black pepper

PARMESAN SAUCE

Mix all ingredients together and refrigerate until ready to serve. *Makes about 1½ cups*

½ cup ricotta cheese

½ cup sour cream

½ cup finely grated Parmesan

¼ cup heavy or whipping cream

1–2 cloves garlic, very finely minced

1 tablespoon very finely minced fresh basil

Salt and freshly coarse-ground black pepper

SAUCE DIJON

Makes about 1 cup

Mix all ingredients together and refrigerate until ready to serve.

1 cup mayonnaise (page 87) or commercial

6–8 cloves garlic, very, very finely minced

3 tablespoons sweet and hot brown mustard (page 86) or commercial

1 tablespoon finely minced fresh parsley

Salt and freshly coarse-ground black pepper

TO ASSEMBLE: Set the prepared artichokes on a serving plate. Gently spread the leaves apart to make the hollow space in the center a bit larger. Fill the center cavity of each artichoke with one of the dips. Garnish the plate with sprigs of fresh herbs and lemon wedges. Your guests will pull off a leaf and dip it the sauce in the center. Be sure to provide a basket or bowl for the discarded leaves.

Some Additional Dipping Sauces for Artichokes

xxxxx

Makes about 1 cup

QUICK AND EASY AIOLI

Put all ingredients into the jar of a blender and process until smooth. Serve chilled.

1 cup mayonnaise (page 87) or commercial

6 large cloves garlic, very finely minced

¼ cup fresh white bread crumbs

Dash of Worcestershire sauce

If you have time to make the real thing see page 85.

ROASTED GARLIC DIP

Makes about 1 cup

Mix all ingredients together well and serve chilled.

½ cup mayonnaise

½ cup sour cream

8–10 cloves roasted garlic (page 83), very finely minced

½ anchovy fillet, very finely minced

Salt and freshly coarse-ground black pepper

HERBED MAYONNAISE

Mix all ingredients together well and serve chilled.

Makes about 1 cup

1 cup mayonnaise

1 tablespoon finely minced fresh dill weed

1 tablespoon finely minced fresh basil

2 tablespoons finely minced fresh chives

¼ cup finely minced sweet purple onion

1 large clove garlic, finely minced

Salt and freshly coarse-ground black pepper

Artichoke Heart Dip

xxxxxx

Makes about 1½ cups

The hearts from 2 or 3 cooked artichokes, chopped

½ cup mayonnaise

½ cup sour cream

¼ cup grated Parmesan

Salt and freshly coarse-ground black pepper

Put artichoke hearts, mayonnaise, and sour cream into the jar of a blender and process until smooth. Remove to a bowl and blend in the Parmesan. Season to taste with salt and pepper and serve chilled.

Artichoke Canapé Tray

xxxxxx

Serves 6–10

1 or 2 large artichokes

½ cup mayonnaise (page 87) or commercial

½ cup sour cream

¼ cup grated Parmesan

2–3 cloves roasted garlic, very finely minced

Worcestershire sauce

Salt and pepper

SUGGESTED GARNISHES:

Cooked baby shrimp meat

Pitted black olive slices

Marinated button mushrooms

Strips of roasted and marinated red bell peppers

Slices of hard-boiled egg

Pickled cocktail onions

Caviar

Caper-stuffed anchovy fillets

This is a supremely easy way to make an attractive canapé tray. Again, the leaves of the artichoke act as vehicles for transporting favorite tidbits to your mouth.

Trim, cook, and drain the artichokes (page 11). Remove the leaves from each artichoke, discarding the very small outer ones and the thin and flimsy inner ones. Set the remaining leaves aside. Remove the choke from the heart (page 13). Mince the heart and put into the jar of your blender with the mayonnaise, sour cream, Parmesan, and garlic, and puree. Remove to a mixing bowl and season to taste with the Worcestershire sauce, salt, and pepper. Set aside. Lay the reserved artichoke leaves on an attractive serving plate in concentric circles. Put a dollop of the mayonnaise/sour cream mixture on each leaf. Use several of the suggested garnishes to top each leaf. Serve chilled.

Artichoke and Olive Tartlets

xxxxxx

Talk about a party in your mouth. You may want to make a double batch because these little nuggets of joy will do an instant disappearing act.

Make your pastry and chill in refrigerator. Preheat oven to 350 degrees F. Heat the olive oil in a heavy skillet and gently sauté the onion and garlic until soft, pinkish, and translucent but not yet beginning to brown. Remove to a bowl and allow to cool. Finely dice the artichoke hearts and add to bowl. Add remaining ingredients and mix well.

Remove the pastry from the refrigerator and roll to a thickness of ¼ inch. Cut into 3½–4-inch disks and use to line the bottoms of standard 2½-inch muffin pans. Spoon the mixture into the pastry shells. Bake in preheated oven for 20–25 minutes or until a toothpick inserted in the center comes out clean. Allow to sit in the pans for about 5 minutes before removing. These tasty tidbits may be served warm or room temperature. For an additional enhancement, add dollops of sour cream as a garnish.

Makes about 24

Your favorite pastry or my perfect pastry recipe (page 82)

2 tablespoons olive oil

About ½ cup finely chopped yellow onion

2 cloves garlic, very finely minced

3–4 large cooked artichoke hearts

¼ cup chopped black olives

½ cup grated sharp Cheddar

½ cup grated mozzarella

2 eggs, lightly beaten

1 cup cream

2 tablespoons sweet and hot brown mustard (page 86) or commercial

2 cloves garlic, very finely minced

½ teaspoon ground nutmeg

¼ cup finely minced fresh parsley

Dash of Worcestershire sauce

Salt and freshly coarse-ground black pepper, to taste

Artichoke and Mushroom Tower

xxxxxx

Serves 4

4 large artichokes

1 yellow onion

1–2 tablespoons olive oil

8 large mushrooms, 2 inches or more (use large white mushrooms, not portobello)

1 cup chicken stock

½ teaspoon mixed dry herbs (Italian seasoning)

2–3 cloves garlic, crushed

1 bay leaf

2 teaspoons paprika

1 tablespoon butter

Loaf of sourdough French or Italian bread

Additional olive oil

2–3 cloves garlic

4 thin slices mozzarella

Curls of fresh Parmesan

Capers

Chopped fresh parsley

Crushed black pepper

Try this unusual tidbit for the perfect start to an elegant meal or as a light and distinctive lunch.

Trim, cook, and drain the artichokes (page 11), and set aside. Preheat oven to 350 degrees F. Peel the onion and slice off 4 sets of rings that are about ½-inch thick. Put the olive oil in a heavy skillet over medium heat. Add the onion rings and sauté gently until they are golden brown, soft, and caramelized but not falling apart, about 3 or 4 minutes. Set aside and keep warm. Peel and trim the mushrooms to form 8 thick slices. Save the trimmings. Gently sauté the mushrooms in the skillet until they are tender and golden brown on each side. Set aside.

Remove the leaves and choke from the artichokes. Save the remaining leaves to use for something else. Trim the hearts so they sit flat, then brown them in the skillet, adding a few more drops of olive oil if necessary.

Add the chicken stock, herbs, garlic, bay leaf, and paprika to the skillet. Add the mushroom trimmings and bring to a boil. Continue to boil until the amount of liquid is reduced by half. Strain and return to the skillet. Add the butter and continue to cook until butter is melted. Keep warm.

Cut 4 slices of sourdough French or Italian bread and then cut into rounds that are a bit larger in circumference than the artichoke hearts. Add a bit of olive oil to a clean skillet and toast the bread on each side. When it is nicely browned, cut garlic cloves in half and rub on both sides of the toast rounds. Place the rounds on a baking sheet. Top each toast round with a slice of the caramelized onion, then top with a mushroom, then an artichoke heart, and top the artichoke heart with another mushroom. Finish off with a slice of mozzarella.* Put into the oven just until the cheese begins to melt and brown. Remove from the oven. Lift each tower onto a serving plate. Pour a bit of the reduced liquid over each one and top with a few shavings of fresh Parmesan. Scatter on a few capers and a bit of fresh parsley and finish with a bit of crushed black pepper.

* You may find it necessary to use a toothpick or short skewer to keep these little towers together.

Artichoke Terrine

xxxxxx

Makes 6–8 servings

1 carton (32 ounces) ricotta cheese

2 envelopes unflavored gelatin

About 2 cups chicken broth or 1 can (14½ ounces)

2 tablespoons sweet and hot brown mustard (page 86) or commercial

1 large or 2 medium leeks

2 roasted sweet red peppers (page 84) or commercial

1–2 portobello mushrooms

1–2 tablespoons olive oil

12–15 large cloves roasted garlic (page 83) or commercial, finely minced

Freshly coarse-ground black pepper

1 can (2¼ ounces) sliced black olives, drained

Hearts from 3–4 large cooked artichokes

Capers

Fresh dill weed, for garnish

This is an elegant and refreshing dish. It makes an excellent addition to a party buffet or may double as a light luncheon salad. It is somewhat labor-intensive, taking three days to make, but for special occasions it is well worth the trouble.

PREPARATIONS: The day before assembling the terrine, line a strainer or colander with soft muslin or a doubled piece of cheesecloth and add the ricotta. Cover with the cloth and put a weight on top. Allow to drip overnight at room temperature. Occasionally press on the weight to try and get out as much moisture as possible.

Reconstitute the unflavored gelatin with the chicken broth, following the manufacturer's directions. Stir in the mustard and set aside.

Trim off the white part of the leeks and reserve.* Wash the green part of the leeks thoroughly. Bring a pot of water to boil and add the leeks. Continue to boil for 3 or 4 minutes or until tender. Remove from boiling water and immediately put into cold water. Drain well. Set aside.

If you are roasting your own peppers, after roasting, remove the seeds and trim, then cut into thin julienne.

Slice the mushrooms into ¼-inch slices. Heat the olive oil in a heavy skillet and gently sauté the mushrooms until they are golden and tender, about 2–3 minutes. Set aside.

* The white of the leek may be sautéed and used in omelets, stir fries, or scrambles; to season stocks; or in any way you would use onion.

TO ASSEMBLE: Line a standard 9 x 5 x 2½-inch Pyrex loaf pan with plastic wrap, allowing about 4 to 6 inches to hang over each long side. Separate the leaves of the leeks and use them to line the loaf pan as well, again leaving several inches of leek hanging over the long sides of the pan. Gently spread a ½-inch layer of ricotta cheese over the bottom of the pan. Sprinkle this with about one-third of the minced roasted garlic and some black pepper. Scatter half of the olive slices over this and top with half the slices of roasted pepper. Add a bit more black pepper and top with half the mushroom slices. Cover the mushrooms with the artichoke hearts and sprinkle with another one-third of the minced roasted garlic. Now you will reverse the process by covering the artichoke hearts with the remaining mushroom slices, topping them with the remaining roasted peppers, then with the remaining olives, sprinkling the remaining roasted garlic over the olives, adding some black pepper and spreading a layer of ricotta over the top.

Now, pour in as much of the gelatin and chicken broth as the dish will hold. To make sure that broth gets all the way through the dish, pour slowly and insert a slim-bladed knife here and there. If the gelatin has congealed, you may heat it for a few seconds in the microwave to reliquefy it. Fold the ends of the leeks over the top of the dish and then fold the plastic wrap over that. Set the pan in another larger dish to catch any drips and put a weight on top. Refrigerate for 2–3 hours or overnight. Save the remaining jelly-broth.

PRESENTATION: To serve, remove from the refrigerator, peel back the plastic wrap from the top, and place a serving dish on top of the pan. Quickly and carefully invert the pan and plate. The terrine should slip out easily. Peel off the plastic wrap. Reliquefy the remaining broth and slowly pour some of it over the terrine, allowing it to form a puddle on the plate. Scatter a few capers over the top and onto the plate. Refrigerate. When the broth has set, remove the terrine from the refrigerator and pour a bit more broth over the top. Refrigerate until set. Continue doing this until the capers are encased in gelatin. To serve, garnish the plate with sprigs of fresh dill weed. Slice into ½-inch slices with a very sharp knife.

Artichoke Torta

xxxxxx

Serves 10–12 as a snack, 6 as a meal

This is a delicious dish that may be cut into small servings and used as party munchies or served as a light meal.

1–2 tablespoons olive oil

1 yellow onion, sliced into thin rings

4–6 cloves garlic, sliced thin

1 large sweet red pepper, seeded and cut into julienne (thin strips)

About 1 cup sliced mushrooms

1 bag (8 ounces) frozen artichoke hearts or 1 can water-pack, drained *

Preheat oven to 350 degrees F. Heat the 1–2 tablespoons of olive oil in a heavy skillet. Over a moderate heat, gently sauté the onion rings and garlic until golden brown. Remove and allow to cool. Sauté the pepper until soft. Remove and allow to cool as well. Sauté the mushrooms until soft and translucent. You may need to add a bit more oil. Remove and allow to cool. Thaw or drain the artichokes and depending on their size, cut in halves or quarters. Dice the drained sun-dried tomatoes. Toss the Cheddar, mozzarella, parsley, and basil together with salt and pepper, to taste.

Unfold one of the thawed sheets of puff pastry and gently roll with a rolling pin until it is half its original thickness. Use

(Ingredients continued on page 27)

STARTERS AND PARTY MUNCHIES **27**

this to line the bottom and sides of a 9-inch springform pan. Line the bottom of the pan with the artichoke hearts. Sprinkle with the ricotta. Cover with the sautéed onion and garlic, the mushrooms, and the peppers. Cover this with the sun-dried tomatoes. Sprinkle the olives over this and top with the sliced hard-boiled eggs. Drizzle with about ¼ cup of olive oil. Top with the cheeses and herbs.

Roll out the second sheet of pastry and cut a circle 10 inches in diameter. Place this over the ingredients in the pan and press down all around the edge. Paint the top with the beaten egg. Cut a 1-inch-diameter hole in the center. Cut leaves from the pastry scraps and use to decorate the top of the torta. Paint the leaves with egg wash as well. Put in the center of the preheated oven with a baking sheet on the rack below to catch any drips. Bake for about 30 minutes or until the pastry is golden brown. Allow to sit in the pan for about 5 minutes before removing to a serving dish. Garnish with sprigs of fresh parsley. This dish is best served at room temperature.

* The size of the can varies from brand to brand; however, most brands are around 14 ounces. You should use about 1 cup and can choose either canned or frozen. The canned might have a bit of an acidic taste; the frozen can be a bit mushy.

** Most brands come in 17.3-ounce boxes containing 2 sheets of pastry. Allow the box to thaw at room temperature. If you don't use both sheets you may reseal the box and refreeze.

About ¼ cup drained sun-dried tomatoes in oil

½ cup grated extra sharp white Cheddar

½ cup grated mozzarella

½ cup minced fresh parsley

¼ cup minced fresh basil leaves

Salt and freshly coarse-ground black pepper

Commercial frozen puff pastry, thawed**

½ cup ricotta cheese

1 can (2¼ ounces) sliced black olives

4 large eggs, hard-boiled, peeled and sliced

¼ cup olive oil

1 raw egg beaten with 1 tablespoon cold water

Sprigs of fresh parsley, for garnish

Artichoke Crostini

xxxxxx

Serves 4–6

1 jar (6 ounces) marinated artichoke hearts, drained and chopped

4–6 cloves roasted garlic (page 83), minced

1 green onion, finely chopped, including most of the green

1 medium tomato, finely diced

¼ cup minced fresh parsley

1 tablespoon capers, rinsed and chopped

2–3 tablespoons chopped black olives

½ cup grated fresh Parmesan

2 tablespoons olive oil

Salt and freshly coarse-ground black pepper

1 baguette, cut into ½-inch slices and toasted on one side

Okay. Okay. So some of the other recipes were a bit tedious to prepare. Here is an easy and incredibly delicious one.

Mix all ingredients except bread together well. Place about a tablespoon of the mixture on the untoasted side of each slice of bread and place under the broiler for about 2 minutes or until the cheese begins to melt. Serve hot.

Artichoke-Stuffed Mushrooms

xxxxxx

Makes 24

24 perfect mushrooms, each about 2 inches in diameter

2–3 strips lean bacon

1 jar (6 ounces) marinated artichoke hearts, drained and well rinsed

¼ cup minced yellow onion

(Ingredients continued on page 29)

This is a real showstopper, and a perfect party dish. Forget the same ol' bean dip or cocktail franks. This one gets rave reviews.

Remove the stems from the mushrooms. Drop the caps into rapidly boiling water and leave for 30 seconds. Remove, plunge into cold water, and drain well. Reserve the stems to flavor stock. Sauté the bacon until crisp. Drain well and set aside. Drain and rinse the artichoke hearts and chop fine. Place in a bowl with the onion, garlic, cheeses, bread crumbs, and parsley. Season to taste with salt and pepper. Add the egg and mix well. Pack this into the mushroom caps. Crumble the bacon and sprinkle a bit on top of each stuffed mushroom. Sprinkle with Parmesan and pop under the broiler only until the cheeses begin to melt, about 2 minutes. Place on a serving plate, garnish with sprigs of fresh parsley, and serve warm.

4 large cloves roasted garlic (page 83), finely minced

½ cup grated sharp Cheddar

½ cup grated Swiss cheese

½ cup fresh bread crumbs

¼ cup finely minced fresh parsley

Salt and freshly coarse-ground black pepper

1 raw egg, lightly beaten

Grated Parmesan

Fresh parsley sprigs, for garnish

Artichoke, Portobello, and Seafood Melt

xxxxxx

Serves 4

This unusual dish may be used as a starter or a light meal. Either way it will provide a touch of elegance, and the bonus is that it is so easy.

Bring a large pot of water to boil and drop the mushrooms in, one at a time, leaving each one in for no more than 30 seconds. As you remove each one, wrap it in a clean tea towel and drain well. When all mushrooms have been blanched, press them lightly in the tea towel to remove as much of the water as possible, because mushrooms act like sponges. Spread the inside of each mushroom with the mustard, then scatter on the minced roasted garlic. Sprinkle with a bit of dill weed, salt, and pepper. Divide the crab or shrimp between the four mushrooms and drizzle on a bit of olive oil. Top each with an artichoke heart. Sprinkle with salt and pepper and top each with a slice of mozzarella. Shake on a bit each of Parmesan and

4 portobello mushrooms

1 tablespoon sweet and hot brown mustard (page 86)

6–8 cloves roasted garlic (page 83), finely minced

Minced fresh dill weed

Salt and freshly coarse-ground black pepper

1 cup chopped cooked fresh crabmeat or baby shrimp meat

Olive oil

The hearts from 4 large cooked artichokes

4 slices mozzarella

Grated Parmesan

Paprika

Sprigs of fresh dill weed, for garnish

Lemon wedges, for garnish

paprika. Put the mushrooms on a baking sheet and place under the broiler until the cheese is melted and beginning to brown, 2–3 minutes. Remove to individual serving plates and garnish with sprigs of fresh dill weed and wedges of lemon.

Marinated Artichokes

xxxxx

Makes 24

Make this when you are lucky enough to find bags of baby artichokes, each about the size of a large hen's egg.

24 baby artichokes

2 cups cider vinegar

¼ cup salt

½ cup sugar

1 tablespoon pickling spice mix

½ teaspoon crushed black peppercorns

½ teaspoon dry dill weed

1 medium yellow onion, cut into thin rings

8–10 cloves garlic, crushed

1 small dry hot chile

¼ cup olive oil

Additional cider vinegar

Steam or boil the artichokes until a leaf comes off easily. Drain well and set aside. Put the 2 cups of cider vinegar, salt, sugar, pickling spice, pepper, and dill weed in a large saucepan and bring to the boil. Reduce heat and simmer for about 10 minutes. Remove from heat and cool. Put the artichokes into a sterilized glass or plastic jar or a ceramic crock large enough to hold them comfortably. Add the onion rings, garlic, chile, and olive oil. Pour the seasoned vinegar over them. Add enough additional vinegar to completely cover the artichokes. Stir gently with a wooden spoon to distribute the ingredients. Cover with a clean cloth, a dish, or a loose-fitting lid and let sit for 2–3 days before using. After tasting, you may add a bit more salt or sugar if you wish. This will keep for at least a month in the pantry, or indefinitely in the refrigerator.

Artichoke and Filo Triangles

xxxxxx

The filo used in this recipe gives California artichokes a Middle Eastern flavor.

Allow package of filo to thaw at room temperature. Chop the artichoke hearts very small. Add the remaining ingredients except olive oil, butter, filo, and vegetable oil. Mix well and set aside.

Remove one end of the roll of filo from its wrapper and cut off a piece 2½ inches wide. Rewrap the remaining dough and return to its box. Refrigerate. Wring a clean tea towel out in cold water. Make sure all the excess moisture is removed; it should be just barely damp. Unroll the strip of filo and lay the moist towel over it. Melt the butter and olive oil together in a small pan.

You will need to work on a flat surface. Lift the cloth and pick up about 3 of the sheets of filo. Lay them on top of each other on your work surface, extending away from you. With a pastry brush, brush the top sheet of filo with the olive oil/butter mixture. Place a teaspoonful of the artichoke/cheese mixture on the end of the pastry nearest you. Now, pretend you are a Boy Scout and fold the pastry up into a triangle in the same way the flag is folded, over and over. You should wind up with a little triangular filo pillow with the stuffing in the center. Place the triangles on a tray or dish, folded seam side down. Repeat until you run out of filling or pastry. You can cut off a new piece of pastry if the first piece wasn't enough.

Heat about ¼ inch of vegetable oil in a heavy skillet and test one of the filo triangles for proper temperature. The filo should turn

Makes about 24

Frozen filo dough*

1 jar (6 ounces) marinated artichoke hearts, drained and rinsed

¼ cup finely chopped sweet red onion

4–6 cloves garlic, finely minced

2 tablespoons finely minced fresh dill weed

2 tablespoons chopped black olives

½ cup crumbled feta cheese

½ cup grated extra sharp Cheddar

Salt and freshly coarse-ground black pepper

¼ cup olive oil

¼ cup butter

Vegetable oil for frying

golden brown in about a minute. When oil is the correct temperature, fry the triangles 5 or 6 at a time for about 1 minute on each side, or until golden brown. Remove to paper towels or a brown paper bag. Serve warm or at room temperature.

* Most brands of filo come in 16-ounce boxes that contain numerous sheets. You will not use an entire box for this recipe. Carefully seal the unused portion and refreeze.

Deep-fried Artichoke Hearts

xxxxxx

Makes about 24

2 cans (14 ounces each) of water-pack artichoke hearts or 2 bags (8 ounces each) frozen ones

Vegetable oil for frying

2–3 eggs, lightly beaten

2 cups well-seasoned bread crumbs

Grated Parmesan

Ranch dressing

This California classic is a long-standing tradition in Castroville and the surrounding area. Not reserved for just upscale restaurants, deep-fried artichoke hearts are found in cafés, diners, pubs, and even the local roach coaches. I much prefer this version to the batter-fried one.

Drain the artichoke hearts well and pat dry. Heat about 3 inches of oil to proper temperature for deep-frying, between 355 and 365 degrees F. Place the beaten eggs and bread crumbs in separate shallow bowls. Dip the drained artichoke hearts, a few at a time, in the beaten eggs. Shake off any excess and dredge by rolling in the seasoned crumbs. Gently slide 3 or 4 dipped and dredged artichoke hearts into the hot oil and fry for 2 or 3 minutes or until golden brown. Using a wooden spoon or long chopsticks, turn them once to guarantee even frying. Remove from the hot oil with a slotted spoon and drain on a wire rack, paper towels, or brown paper bag. Keep warm. Continue until all the hearts are cooked. Place on a serving dish and sprinkle with Parmesan and accompany with ranch dressing for dipping.

Soup, Beautiful Soup

xxxxxx

Curried Artichoke Soup

xxxxxx

Try this unusual soup when you want a touch of the exotic. It features a whisper of curry.

Serves 4–6

3–4 tablespoons olive oil

1 tablespoon curry powder

1 medium-size yellow onion, sliced into thin rings

4–6 cloves garlic, thinly sliced

1–2 thin slices fresh ginger root, very finely minced

About 2 cups frozen or canned (water-pack) artichoke hearts, drained

Dry chile flakes

Salt and freshly coarse-ground black pepper

About 6 cups or 1 can (49½ ounces) chicken broth

Fresh cilantro, chopped, for garnish

Heat the olive oil in a heavy skillet over moderate heat. Add the curry, onion, garlic, and ginger and sauté until the onions are soft and translucent, 2 to 3 minutes. Depending on the size, halve or quarter the artichoke hearts and add to the skillet. Add the chile flakes to taste and sauté until the artichoke hearts are hot through and well coated with the curry-flavored oil. Season to taste with salt and pepper. Set aside and keep warm. In a large pot, heat the chicken broth to the simmer point. Divide the artichoke mixture between individual serving bowls and ladle the hot broth over the mixture. Scatter a bit of chopped cilantro on top and serve hot.

Artichoke and Prawn Soup

xxxxxx

Serves 4–6

1 tablespoon olive oil

1 medium-size
onion, chopped

4–6 cloves garlic, chopped

1 pound fresh prawns

¼ cup inexpensive
cream Sherry

1 can (14 ounces) water-pack
artichoke hearts, drained,
liquid reserved

1 can (49½-ounces) chicken
broth, about 6 cups

1 teaspoon Italian seasoning

Salt and freshly coarse-
ground black pepper

Sesame oil

Fresh cilantro, for garnish

This simple yet sophisticated soup may be served hot or chilled, thus bringing elegance to your table all year round.

Heat the olive oil in a large heavy pot and gently sauté the onion and garlic until pinkish and translucent. Add the prawns and continue to sauté until the prawns turn pink.

Remove all from the skillet and set aside. Deglaze the pan with the Sherry. Add the liquid from the artichokes and the chicken broth to the pan and bring to a boil. Reduce heat to a simmer. Peel the prawns and reserve the meat. Add the shells, onion, and garlic to the simmering broth. Add the Italian seasoning.

Continue to simmer for about 20 minutes, then strain and return to the pot. Season to taste with salt and pepper. Coarsely chop the prawns and artichoke hearts. Divide the prawns and artichoke hearts between the number of individual serving bowls being used. Ladle the broth over the prawns and artichoke hearts and add a drop of sesame oil to each serving. Garnish each serving with a sprig of fresh cilantro.

Cream of Artichoke Heart Soup

xxxxxx

This delicious and comforting soup is a good way to use up the stems and leaves from artichokes that you have used in other recipes.

Trim, cook, and drain the artichokes (page 11). Put chicken broth, onion, garlic, Italian seasoning, and nutmeg into a large pot and bring to the boil. Reduce the temperature and continue to simmer. When artichokes are cool enough to handle, remove the leaves, chokes, and stems and put into the pot with the chicken broth. Dice the hearts and set aside. Continue to simmer the broth, leaves, chokes, and stems for about 30 minutes. Allow to cool a bit. Strain and return the broth to the pot. Press the solid material with the back of a spoon to extract as much liquid as possible and return the liquid to the pot. Put the hearts into a blender with 1 cup of broth and blend. Return to the pot. Add the cream and Sherry and heat to serving temperature. Season to taste with salt and pepper. Add a dollop of sour cream and a sprinkling of chopped parsley to each serving.

Serves 4–6

4 large artichokes

2 cans (14½ ounces each) chicken broth

1 large onion, chopped

4–6 cloves garlic, chopped

1 teaspoon Italian seasoning

½ teaspoon ground nutmeg

2 cups cream or half-and-half

¼ cup inexpensive cream Sherry

Salt and freshly coarse-ground black pepper

Sour cream

Chopped fresh parsley

Roasted Garlic and Artichoke Soup
xxxxxx

Serves 4–6

1 can (49⅛ ounces) chicken broth

1 can (14 ounces) water-pack artichoke hearts, drained and diced, liquid reserved

6–8 cloves roasted garlic (page 83), minced

½ teaspoon ground nutmeg

1 teaspoon Italian seasoning

¼ cup inexpensive cream Sherry

½ cup grated Swiss cheese

½ cup grated Cheddar

¼ cup finely chopped fresh parsley

4–6 slices French bread, ½-inch thick

2 tablespoons sweet and hot brown mustard (page 86)

4–6 additional cloves roasted garlic, minced

Castroville has its Artichoke Festival and Gilroy has its Garlic Festival. These two California communities are only 20 miles apart. This robust soup might well be appropriately served at either festival. Not only is this soup delicious, it is oh, so easy.

Put broth, diced artichokes, reserved artichoke liquid, roasted garlic, nutmeg, and Italian seasoning in a large pot and bring to a boil. Reduce the heat to a simmer and continue to cook for another 20 minutes. Remove from heat and stir in the Sherry. Toss the cheeses together with the parsley. Toast the bread and spread one side of each slice with the brown mustard. Sprinkle each slice with minced roasted garlic. Divide the broth between 4–6 heatproof serving bowls. Float a toast raft in each bowl and sprinkle the raft generously with the cheeses. Put under the broiler just until the cheese melts and begins to bubble. Serve hot.

Artichoke and Mushroom Soup

xxxxxx

This light and delicious soup is just the thing for springtime, when the hearty soups of winter are no longer appropriate but there is still a chill in the evening air.

Trim the artichokes (page 11). Save the trimmings. Cut the stems off the mushrooms and save. Put the artichokes and trimmings, mushroom stems, onion, garlic, Italian seasoning, and chicken broth into a large pot and bring to the boil. Reduce the heat to a rapid simmer and continue to cook until you can easily pull a leaf off the artichokes. Remove from heat. When cool enough to handle, remove all the leaves from the artichokes and return the leaves to the pot. Remove and discard the chokes (page 13). Reserve the hearts. Return the pot to the stove and continue to simmer covered for 20–30 minutes. Allow to cool slightly for safety's sake, then strain. Return the broth to the pot.

Slice the mushrooms. Heat the oil and butter together in a heavy skillet and gently sauté the mushrooms for 2–3 minutes or until translucent and just beginning to brown. Add to the broth. Cut the artichoke hearts into julienne and add to the broth as well. Add the Sherry and heat to serving temperature. Season to taste with salt and pepper. Serve in individual soup bowls with a scattering of toasted almonds.

Serves 4–6

3–4 large artichokes

1 pound mushrooms

1 yellow onion, coarsely chopped

4–6 cloves garlic

1 teaspoon Italian seasoning

6 cups or 1 can (49½ ounces) chicken broth

1 tablespoon olive oil

1 tablespoon butter

¼ cup inexpensive cream Sherry

Salt and freshly coarse-ground black pepper

Sliced, toasted almonds

Tuscan Artichoke Heart and Garlic Crouton Salad

xxxxxx

Salads utilizing stale bread are a standard item in Italy. This delicious creation is an excellent example.

Drain the artichoke hearts and reserve the liquid. Depending on their size, cut the artichokes into halves or quarters. Put into a bowl. Add the tomatoes, chopped onion, black olives, croutons, capers, chopped garlic, dill weed, and parsley. Toss well. Measure the liquid from the artichokes and, if needed, add enough olive oil to bring the total to ½ cup. Blend in the mustard. Pour over the salad and toss well. Season to taste with salt and pepper. Refrigerate for at least an hour before serving. Serve on a bed of romaine lettuce and top generously with curls of fresh Parmesan or Romano cheese.

Serves 4–6

2–3 jars (6 ounces each) marinated artichoke hearts

3–4 large very ripe tomatoes, diced

1 medium-size sweet purple onion, ½ chopped fine, ½ cut into thin rings

About ½ cup whole black olives

2 cups garlic croutons

2 teaspoons capers, rinsed

4–6 cloves roasted garlic (page 83), chopped

1 teaspoon finely minced fresh dill weed

2 tablespoons finely chopped fresh parsley

Olive oil

2 tablespoons sweet and hot brown mustard (page 86)

Salt and freshly coarse-ground black pepper

Fresh romaine lettuce

Curls of fresh Parmesan or Romano cheese

Artichoke, Chicken Breast, and Roasted Pepper Salad

xxxxxx

Serves 4

4 large artichokes

2 roasted sweet red peppers (page 84), seeded, trimmed, and cut into julienne

2 grilled boneless chicken breasts, cut into julienne

4–6 cloves roasted garlic (page 83), minced

1 tablespoon chopped chives

About ½ cup finely chopped sweet purple onion

2 tablespoons sweet and hot brown mustard (page 86)

⅓ cup olive oil

⅓ cup red wine vinegar

Salt and freshly coarse-ground black pepper

Thin sweet purple onion rings

This robust yet elegant salad is the very essence of contemporary Western cooking. And it is so easy, even a caveman can make it!

Trim, cook, and drain the artichokes (page 11). When the artichokes are cool enough to handle, remove the leaves and reserve. Remove and discard the choke (page 13). Cut the hearts into thin strips and put into a bowl. Put the peppers, chicken, garlic, chives, and chopped onion into a bowl and toss gently. Blend the mustard, oil, and vinegar together well and pour over the salad. Toss gently. Season to taste with salt and freshly coarse-ground black pepper.

Arrange the meatiest of the artichoke leaves in a circle on four salad plates. Divide the salad between the plates and top with a few thin rings of sweet purple onion.

Artichoke Salad, Sicilian Style

xxxxxx

This robust Sicilian-style salad is the very essence of the Mediterranean. It's enough to make any "Godfather" weep.

Drain the artichoke hearts and cut in halves or quarters, depending on the size. Put into a bowl. Add the drained diced tomatoes. Drain the black olives and crush with the flat of a chef's knife. Add black and Kalamata olives, capers, green and purple onion, garlic, basil, and chopped pepperoncini to the bowl and toss lightly. Arrange a bed of salad greens in individual salad bowls and divide the salad between them. Garnish each plate with a few slices of hard-boiled egg, a pepperoncino, and a sprig of fresh basil. Blend the oil and vinegar together and drizzle over the salads. Season to taste with salt and pepper.

Serves 4–6

2 jars (6 ounces each) marinated artichoke hearts, drained, liquid reserved

1 can (14½ ounces) diced tomatoes, drained

1 cup pitted black olives

½ cup pitted Kalamata olives

1 tablespoon capers

2–3 green onions, chopped, including most of the greens

½ cup chopped sweet purple onion

6–8 cloves roasted garlic (page 86), chopped

¼ cup finely chopped fresh basil leaves

2–3 pickled Italian-style pepperoncini, chopped

Salad greens of choice

2 hard-boiled eggs, sliced, for garnish

Pickled Italian-style pepperoncini, for garnish

Sprigs of fresh basil, for garnish

⅓ cup olive oil

½ cup red wine vinegar

Salt and freshly coarse-ground black pepper

Artichoke Greek Salad

xxxxxx

Serves 4–6

Try this California edition of the Greek classic. I think you will be very pleasantly surprised.

2 jars (6 ounces each) marinated artichoke hearts, drained and cut into halves or quarters, depending on size

2–3 large ripe tomatoes, cut into small wedges

1 small cucumber, peeled, seeded, and diced

1 cup pitted Greek olives or pitted California black olives, left whole

1 cup cubed feta cheese

½ green bell pepper, seeded and cut into thin julienne

1 teaspoon finely chopped fresh Greek or Mediterranean oregano

⅓ cup olive oil

Juice of 2 lemons

1 teaspoon sugar

Salt and freshly coarse-ground black pepper

Romaine lettuce

Combine the first seven ingredients in a bowl. Blend oil, lemon juice, and sugar together well and pour over the salad. Toss gently. Add salt and pepper to taste. Serve on a bed of romaine lettuce.

California Potato Salad

xxxxxx

Serves 4–6

Not the same ol' potato salad. Here is a California twist on the traditional theme. This salad not only makes good use of classically Californian products such as artichokes and olives, it also replaces the usual mayonnaise dressing with a garlic-and-mustard vinaigrette.

Wash the potatoes, place in a large pot, cover with water, bring to a boil, then reduce heat to maintain a rapid simmer until they may be easily pierced with a cooking fork. Drain, and when they are cool enough to handle but still warm, peel them.** Cut into bite-size pieces and place in a large bowl. Add the remaining salad ingredients and toss gently.

Blend the oil, vinegar, mustard, and garlic together in a small bowl and pour over the salad. Gently toss again. Season to taste with salt and pepper and chill for at least an hour before serving. To serve, line a salad bowl with lettuce and pile the salad on top of it. Top with freshly grated Parmesan or Romano.

* If you like the taste of the marinade you may use it as part of the vinaigrette.

** Never peel potatoes before boiling when making potato salad or mashed potatoes. It makes them watery.

SALAD:

2–3 large potatoes

2 jars (6 ounces each) marinated artichoke hearts, drained *

1 rib celery, chopped

2–3 green onions, chopped, including most of the green

1 medium-size sweet purple onion, diced

½ sweet red bell pepper, seeded and cut into thin julienne

1 cup pitted black olives, crushed

¼ cup sweet pickle relish

1 tablespoon finely minced fresh dill weed

¼ cup chopped fresh parsley

1 tablespoon capers (optional)

VINAIGRETTE:

⅓ cup olive oil

½ cup cider vinegar

2 tablespoons sweet and hot brown mustard (page 86)

4–6 cloves garlic, very finely minced

Salt and freshly coarse-ground black pepper

Crisp lettuce

Freshly grated Parmesan or Romano cheese

Serves 4

Artichoke Louis

xxxxxx

4 large artichokes

SALAD:

2 cups flaked crabmeat

½ cup finely chopped celery

½ cup finely chopped sweet purple onion

1 cup shredded crisp iceberg lettuce

¼ cup sliced black olives

¼ cup finely chopped parsley

1 tablespoon finely chopped fresh dill weed

DRESSING:

⅔ cup mayonnaise (page 87), or commercial

¼ cup chile sauce or ketchup

1 tablespoon fresh lemon juice

1 teaspoon Worcestershire sauce

1 teaspoon prepared horseradish, or to taste

Salt and freshly coarse-ground black pepper

GARNISH:

2 Roma tomatoes, cut into wedges

4 hard-boiled eggs, peeled and sliced

Thin sweet purple onion rings

Sprigs of fresh dill weed

Talk about Western! Crab Louis is a thoroughly West Coast invention, having been created shortly after 1900 to showcase our magnificent Dungeness crabs. Both Seattle and San Francisco claim to have originated it. Being an adamant Californian, my money is on San Francisco. This recipe cements the San Francisco claim by serving it in an artichoke.

Trim, cook, and drain the artichokes (page 11). When the artichokes are cool enough to handle, remove the flimsy inner leaves and the chokes, (page 13). Chill.

Gently mix all salad ingredients together in a large bowl. Blend the dressing ingredients together and pour over the salad. Toss gently. Season to taste with salt and pepper. Chill. When ready to assemble, set each artichoke on a salad plate and gently spread the remaining leaves apart. Divide the salad between the four plates, piling it into the center of the artichokes. Garnish each plate with several wedges of tomato, slices of hard-boiled egg, a few onion rings, and a sprig of fresh dill weed.

California Pasta and Artichoke Heart Salad *Serves 4–6*

XXXXXX

This tasty recipe employs a variety of choice California products. If available, substitute an equivalent amount of cooked fresh artichoke hearts for the water-pack or frozen ones.

Cook the pasta to your desired degree of doneness and drain well. Set aside. Put the oil, vinegar, ranch dressing, mustard, and garlic in a large bowl and stir well. Add the cooked pasta and toss to coat evenly. Set aside and allow to marinate for about an hour. Toss occasionally to insure all is well coated.

While the pasta is marinating, prepare the remaining ingredients. If using frozen artichoke hearts, blanch them in boiling water until tender, 6–8 minutes. Drain and cool. Cut artichoke hearts into bite-size pieces.

When ready to assemble the salad, remove the pasta to a serving plate. Add the artichoke hearts, diced onion, and next 6 ingredients to the bowl in which the pasta was marinating. Toss gently to coat evenly. Season to taste with salt and pepper and arrange the salad on top of the pasta. Arrange the crab and onion rings on top of the salad. Scatter generously with curls of fresh Parmesan. Drizzle a bit more dressing over all if desired.

About 3 ounces dry fettuccine

⅛ cup olive oil

⅛ cup cider vinegar

½ cup ranch dressing

2 tablespoons sweet and hot brown mustard (page 86)

4–6 cloves roasted garlic (page 83), minced

About 2 cups water-pack or frozen artichoke hearts

1 medium-size sweet purple onion, half diced and half cut into thin rings

1 cup pitted black olives, mashed

¼ cup sun-dried tomatoes in oil, drained and cut into thin slivers

10–12 snow peas, cut into thin julienne

About 1 cup fresh arugula (rocket), rinsed and torn into bite-size pieces

About 2 cups baby romaine, rinsed and torn into bite-size pieces

1 tablespoon finely chopped fresh dill weed

Salt and freshly coarse-ground black pepper

1 cup crabmeat (if crab is not available use cooked baby shrimp meat)

Fresh Parmesan, shaved into curls

Artichoke Salad Niçoise

xxxxxx

Serves 4–6

This classic salad from the south of France provides an excellent vehicle for showing off marinated artichoke hearts. Traditionally it contains fresh green beans. This recipe replaces the beans with our sophisticated thistle.

SALAD:

1 pound tiniest new potatoes

2 jars (6 ounces each) marinated artichoke hearts

2 cans (6 ounces each) oil-pack tuna

Salad greens

2–3 tomatoes, cut into wedges

2–3 hard-boiled eggs, cut into wedges

About ½ cup pitted Niçoise, Kalamata, or black olives, or combination thereof

1 tablespoon capers

2–3 anchovy fillets, minced

Thin sweet purple onion rings

Clipped fresh dill weed

Clipped fresh tarragon

Cracked black pepper

DRESSING:

Marinade from artichokes

Oil from tuna

3–4 cloves garlic, finely minced

1 tablespoon sweet and hot brown mustard (page 86)

Red wine vinegar

Wash but do not peel the potatoes. Place in cold water, bring to a boil, reduce heat to maintain a gentle boil, and continue to cook until tender. Drain and leave in cold water until completely cold. Drain again. Drain the marinade from the artichokes and the oil from the tuna and reserve both. Dress a serving plate with salad greens of choice. Cut the potatoes in half and arrange in a pile in the center of the dish. Cut the artichoke hearts in half and arrange in a circle around the potatoes. Arrange the wedges of tomato around the artichokes. Next place the wedges of egg around the tomatoes. Being careful not to break it apart, place piles of tuna around the eggs. Scatter the olives over the salad, followed by the capers. Scatter the minced anchovy fillets on top. Strew a few sweet purple onion rings on top and finish by scattering on a bit each of clipped dill weed and tarragon. Finish with cracked black pepper.

Blend the marinade from the artichokes, the oil from the tuna, the garlic, and the mustard together well. Add enough red wine vinegar to make ½ cup total. Sprinkle this over the salad. Serve chilled.

Artichoke Hearts and Seafood Linguine

xxxxxx

Serves 4–6

Pasta, seafood, and artichoke hearts come together to make this sunny, Mediterranean classic.

About 8 ounces dry linguine

A few drops olive oil

1–2 tablespoons additional olive oil

1 medium-size yellow onion, diced

6–8 cloves garlic, sliced thin

1 can (14 ounces) water-pack artichoke hearts, drained and cut into bite-size pieces

2–3 ripe tomatoes, diced

½ teaspoon Italian seasoning

1 can (6½ ounces) minced or chopped clams

¼ cup dry red wine

½ cup chopped fresh basil leaves

1 cup cooked baby shrimp meat

Salt and freshly coarse-ground black pepper

Sprigs of fresh basil, for garnish

Cook the pasta to desired degree of doneness and drain well. Add a few drops of olive oil and toss gently. Cover and set aside.

Heat 1 or 2 tablespoons of olive oil in a heavy skillet and gently sauté the onion and garlic until soft, translucent, and just beginning to brown around the edges. Add the artichokes and continue to sauté for 2 or 3 minutes or until just beginning to brown around the edges. Add the tomatoes, Italian seasoning, juice from the clams, and wine, and simmer for about 5 minutes. Add the clams, basil, and shrimp, and continue to simmer for another 2 or 3 minutes or until all is hot through. Season to taste with salt and pepper. Place the pasta on a serving dish and pour the artichoke and seafood sauce over it. Garnish with sprigs of fresh basil.

Artichoke Heart, Olive, and Roasted Garlic Pizza

XXXXXX

If there is anyone who doesn't like pizza, I haven't met them yet. Here is a red-sauce pizza based on a Sicilian classic, and it's so easy. You start with ready-to-use products and add a few homemade touches.

Follow the manufacturer's instructions for thawing the pizza dough. Preheat oven to 500 degrees F. Heat the olive oil in a heavy skillet and gently sauté the onion and mushrooms until heated through and translucent but not yet beginning to brown. Place the pizza dough on a pan and spread generously with the sauce. Sprinkle the sautéed onions and mushrooms evenly over the top. Continue scattering the remaining ingredients except cheese over the pizza. Gently toss the mozzarella and Cheddar together and scatter evenly over the pizza, then top with the Parmesan. Bake for 20–25 minutes or until the bottom of the crust is brown. When removed from the oven, allow to sit for a few minutes before slicing.

Serves 2–3

1 frozen pizza shell (9 or 10 inches)

1–2 tablespoons olive oil

½ yellow onion, diced

1 cup sliced mushrooms

About 2 cups ready-made canned or jarred spaghetti, marinara, or other red sauce

1 jar (6½ ounces) marinated artichoke hearts, drained and chopped

2–3 tablespoons sliced black olives, well drained

8–10 cloves roasted garlic (page 83), chopped

About 2 tablespoons chopped fresh basil

About ½ cup grated mozzarella

About ½ cup grated Cheddar

¼ cup grated Parmesan

Artichoke Heart and Seafood Pizza with Alfredo Sauce

xxxxxx

Serves 2–3

1 frozen pizza shell (9 or 10 inches)

1 jar (16 ounces) Alfredo sauce

About 1 cup well-drained water-pack artichoke hearts, sliced

1 cup cooked baby shrimp meat

1 can (6½ ounces) chopped or minced clams, drained

About ½ cup grated mozzarella

About ½ cup grated fresh Parmesan

1 tablespoon finely chopped fresh parsley

1 teaspoon finely chopped fresh dill weed

Freshly coarse-ground black pepper

Most pizzerias offer an artichoke-and-shrimp pizza with white sauce. I always thought I should like it but never did. I recently realized why. They use marinated artichoke hearts, and to me the vinegar taste overpowers the delicate flavor of the shrimp and white sauce. I much prefer this version using the water-pack artichokes.

Thaw the pizza dough according to the manufacturer's directions. Preheat oven to 500 degrees F. Spread the dough generously with the Alfredo sauce. Sprinkle the top evenly with sliced artichoke hearts, shrimp, and clams. Gently toss the two cheeses and herbs together and sprinkle over the top of the pizza. Season to taste with fresh pepper and bake for about 20 minutes or until the cheeses are bubbling and just beginning to brown. Remove from the oven and allow to sit for a few minutes before cutting.

California Omelet

xxxxxx

Who says omelets have to be for breakfast only? I often serve a beautiful omelet for lunch or dinner. This one sports a variety of fine California products.

If using fresh artichokes, trim, cook, drain, and remove the chokes (pages 11–13), then chop the hearts. If using canned, drain and chop. Break eggs into a small bowl and beat lightly. Set aside and allow any foam to subside. Heat the olive oil in a heavy skillet and gently sauté the onion and garlic until the onion is pinkish and translucent but not yet beginning to brown. Remove to a small bowl and wipe the skillet clean. Wipe the skillet with a bit more olive oil and put over moderate heat.

Drop a small spoonful of the beaten egg into the skillet to test for proper heat. The egg should solidify but not bubble and curl up around the edges. When pan is the proper heat, carefully pour the eggs into it and swirl the pan to coat the bottom evenly. Using the back of a table fork, gently agitate the surface of the egg until it is custard-like and beginning to set, being careful not to disturb the thin skin that will form on the bottom, for about 2 minutes. While the egg is still soft but not runny, sprinkle the cheeses evenly over the surface. Scatter the remaining ingredients, except salt and pepper, evenly over the top and continue to cook gently until the egg is set to your desired degree of doneness. Season to taste with salt and pepper. Carefully fold the omelet in half and continue to cook for a few seconds longer. Then slide it out onto a heated plate and set aside to keep warm while you make the sauce.

Serves 2

Hearts from 2 large cooked artichokes, chopped (if not available substitute an equivalent amount of canned water-pack)

4 eggs

1–2 tablespoons olive oil

About ½ yellow onion, chopped

3–4 cloves garlic, minced

Olive oil

About ⅓ cup grated Swiss cheese

About ⅓ cup grated sharp Cheddar

2 tablespoons drained sliced black olives

About 2 tablespoons roasted sweet red pepper (page 84)

½ cup flaked crabmeat or chopped cooked baby shrimp meat

Salt and freshly coarse-ground black pepper

(Ingredients continued on page 54)

SAUCE AND GARNISHES:

2 tablespoons butter

¼ cup inexpensive
cream Sherry

1 tablespoon sweet and hot
brown mustard (page 86)

2 teaspoons minced fresh
dill weed or ¼ teaspoon dry

Salt and freshly coarse-
ground black pepper

Sour cream (optional)

A few slices of black olive

Slivers of roasted sweet
red pepper

Sprigs of fresh dill weed
or parsley, for garnish

Lemon slices, for garnish

Wipe the pan again and add the butter, Sherry, mustard, and dill weed. Swirl over a moderately high heat until the butter is melted and the liquid has slightly reduced and thickened, about 2–3 minutes. Season to taste with salt and pepper and pour over the omelet. Top with a dollop of sour cream and scatter a few slices of black olive and roasted pepper over the top. Garnish with a sprig of fresh dill weed or parsley and a slice of lemon.

Portobello and Artichoke Hearts Gratin
xxxxxx

Serves 4

4 large artichokes

4 portobello mushrooms

2 tablespoons olive oil

1 medium-size yellow
onion, diced

4–6 cloves garlic, minced

½ teaspoon Italian seasoning

2 ripe tomatoes, diced

1 tablespoon chopped
fresh basil

(Ingredients continued on page 55)

This is a truly delicious and unusual special-occasion dish that is not difficult but looks and tastes as though you ordered it in an exclusive bistro. To make this dish you will, however, need four heatproof dinner plates.

Preheat oven to 350 degrees F. Trim and cook the artichokes (page 11). Cook the stems also, and if they are tender chop and use them as well. Drain the artichokes well and remove all the leaves. Remove and discard the chokes (page 13). Set the hearts and leaves aside. Remove the stems from the portobellos and save for your stock pot. Peel the mushrooms and with a spoon scrape off the gills. Drop into boiling water and cook only until the water returns to a boil. Remove from the water immediately, rinse under cold running water, and set aside to drain.

Heat the olive oil in a heavy skillet and gently sauté the onion and garlic until the onion is translucent and pinkish but not yet beginning to brown. Add the Italian seasoning, tomatoes, and basil. Continue to sauté until the tomatoes have released some of their juice, about 2 minutes. Chop the artichoke hearts and add along with the ham and cook until all is hot through and any liquid absorbed. Set aside.

In a medium pot, blend together the butter and flour and cook over medium heat, stirring all the while until it begins to bubble, but do not let it brown. Add the milk or half-and-half and cook, whisking constantly, until slightly thickened, about 4–5 minutes. Combine the cheeses and reserve about ½ cup. Add the remainder to the white sauce, along with the nutmeg and dill, and continue to cook over low heat, stirring, until the cheeses have melted. Season to taste with salt and pepper.

Wrap the mushrooms in a clean tea towel and press gently to remove any excess water. Place a mushroom on each of 4 heat-proof dinner plates. Pile the artichoke-and-ham mixture onto the 4 mushrooms. Arrange the meatiest of the artichoke leaves in a circle around each mushroom. Pour the cheese sauce over the mushrooms. Sprinkle each with the remaining cheeses and a dash of paprika. Place the four plates into the preheated oven just until the cheeses begin to melt and the tops brown a bit. Serve hot. The diners may scoop up the cheese sauce with the artichoke leaves and eat the stuffed hearts with a knife and fork.

1 cup finely chopped lean cooked ham

1½ tablespoons butter

1½ tablespoons all-purpose flour

1½ cups milk or half-and-half

¾ cup grated mozzarella

¾ cup grated sharp Cheddar

¼ teaspoon ground nutmeg

1 tablespoon minced fresh dill weed or ½ teaspoon dry

Salt and freshly coarse-ground black pepper

Paprika

Roulade of Beef Tenderloin with Castroville Artichoke, Dungeness Crab, and Grilled Spring Vegetables

xxxxxx

Serves 6

2 pounds beef tenderloin

½ tablespoon finely chopped fresh rosemary

½ tablespoon finely chopped fresh thyme

2 artichokes

1 zucchini, sliced into 4 pieces lengthwise (approximately ¼ inch thick)

1 yellow squash, sliced into 4 pieces lengthwise (approximately ¼ inch thick)

1 pound Dungeness crab

2 tablespoons crème fraiche or sour cream

1 tablespoon Dijon mustard

1 teaspoons freshly grated lemon zest

1 tablespoon finely sliced fresh chives

½ cup olive oil

Sea salt and pepper

This recipe was graciously shared by Chef Colin Moody, who served this delicious dish at a Cooking For Solutions organic luncheon in 2007.

Preheat oven to 350 degrees F. Season the beef tenderloin with the chopped rosemary, thyme, salt, and pepper. In an oven-proof sauté pan, place 2 tablespoons of the olive oil, and place over medium-high heat. Put the beef in the pan and brown all sides of the beef evenly (1–2 minutes per side), then place pan in the oven and bake until medium rare (approximately 15–20 minutes), or until it reads 135 degrees on a thermometer. Take out of the oven, let rest at room temperature for 15 minutes, then chill in refrigerator.

Turn on grill or prepare barbecue. Place sliced zucchini and yellow squash in a medium bowl, add remaining olive oil, and salt and pepper to taste. Toss until well coated. Grill zucchini and squash for approximately 2 minutes on each side. Let cool. Cook and drain the artichokes (page 11) and remove the chokes (page 13) and tough outer leaves. Slice zucchini and squash into ½-inch pieces and place in a large mixing bowl. Cut the artichokes into small, bite-size wedges. Place the artichokes in the bowl with the zucchini and squash. Then add the crab, crème fraiche, mustard, lemon zest, chives, and salt and pepper to taste. Mix gently until well incorporated.

Remove the chilled beef tenderloin from the refrigerator. Lay down a large sheet of plastic wrap. Slice the beef a thinly as possible (without tearing it) and lay the pieces of beef overlapping on top of the plastic wrap to form a rectangle that is about 12 x 6 inches. Then mound the crab-vegetable mixture down the center of the beef. Using the plastic wrap to help you, roll the beef around the crab mixture to form a "log." Twist the plastic at both ends of the log and let the "roulade" chill in the refrigerator for at least 2 hours. Remove from the refrigerator and plastic. Then slice to desired thickness and serve with a salad, or serve alone for a fun summer dish!

Chef Colin Moody, CCC, is Executive Chef at Monterey Peninsula Country Club and Chairman of the Board of the American Culinary Federation, Monterey Bay.

Benedict Artichoke

XXXXXX

Makes 4

4 large artichokes

4 slices of lean ham

4 eggs

2 English muffins, split, toasted, and buttered

1½ cups hollandaise sauce (see below)

Paprika

Lemon wedges, for garnish

Of course when you eat hollandaise sauce you can feel your arteries slamming shut with every bite, but please don't even bother trying a low-fat, healthful version. Make the real thing. Pull out all the stops. Just don't eat it more than twice a year.

Trim, cook, and drain the artichokes (page 11). Remove and discard the choke (page 13) and set the leaves and hearts aside. Gently fry or broil the ham and keep warm. Poach the eggs. Place a buttered muffin on each plate. Top with a slice of ham. Top each slice of ham with an artichoke heart and slide a poached egg on top of each. Arrange the meatiest of the artichoke leaves in a circle around the plate and top the creation with the hollandaise sauce. Finish with a light shake of paprika and garnish each plate with a wedge of lemon.

HOLLANDAISE SAUCE

Makes about 1½ cups

3 egg yolks

1 tablespoon fresh lemon juice

2 sticks (½ pound) melted butter

1 tablespoon hot water

Cayenne pepper

Dry dill weed

Salt

Put the egg yolks in a heavy saucepan and beat them with a wire whisk for a minute or 2 or until they become slightly thickened. Beat in the lemon juice. Place the saucepan over low heat and continue to whisk the mixture until it becomes smooth, creamy, and thickened. You can remove the pan from the heat periodically to prevent the mixture from cooking too quickly. Remove from heat and begin adding the butter, about ½ teaspoon at a time, quickly beating in each addition before adding the next. Be sure to scrape down the bottom and sides of the pan as you work. When the mixture is the consistency of heavy cream, you may begin whisking in the butter, about a teaspoon at a time. The total process should take about 5 minutes. When the butter is all added, whisk in the spoonful of hot water. Season to taste with the cayenne pepper, dill weed, and salt.

Hollandaise sauce will not hold for long. You can keep it warm for a short time by placing it over a pot of warm, not hot, water. Despite all efforts, hollandaise sauce will sometimes break or curdle. Sometimes it can be reclaimed by whisking in an additional tablespoon of hot water. Sometimes you can run it through your blender. If it breaks do not blame yourself. Sometimes it happens. Good luck.

Artichoke and Grilled Chicken Breast with Roasted Garlic Sauce

Serves 4

xxxxxx

Here is another totally sinful recipe. You can allow yourself to have it when you have been a really good kid.

Trim, cook, and drain the artichokes, remove the chokes (pages 11–13), and set leaves and hearts aside. Cut each chicken breast in half. Rub with olive oil and mustard. Sprinkle lightly with salt and pepper and grill or broil to desired degree of doneness. The chicken is done when the thickest part is opaque, not translucent, and any juice runs clear, not pink. Set aside and keep warm.

Make the hollandaise sauce and at the last minute whisk in the minced garlic and dill weed. Place an artichoke heart on each plate. Lay a piece of chicken breast on top of each and arrange the meatiest of the leaves around it. Top each with a generous dollop of hollandaise sauce. Garnish each plate with a light sprinkling of paprika, a sprig of dill weed, and a wedge of lemon.

4 large artichokes

2 large boneless chicken breasts

Olive oil

About 1 tablespoon Dijon mustard

Salt and freshly coarse-ground black pepper

Hollandaise sauce (page 58)

6–8 cloves roasted garlic (page 83), finely minced

About 1 teaspoon finely minced fresh dill weed

Paprika, for garnish

Sprigs of fresh dill weed, for garnish

Wedges of lemon, for garnish

Couscous-stuffed Artichokes

xxxxxx

Serves 4

4 large artichokes

1 can (14½ ounces or about 2 cups) chicken broth

1 cup instant couscous

1 tablespoon olive oil

1 medium-size onion, coarsely chopped

3–4 cloves garlic, minced

1 ripe tomato, diced

1 teaspoon curry powder

½ teaspoon dry dill weed

½ teaspoon ground cumin

¼ cup currants

¼ cup pine nuts or slivered almonds

1 teaspoon sugar

1 green onion, finely chopped, including most of the green

The juice and zest of 1 lemon

2–3 tablespoons additional olive oil

Salt and freshly coarse-ground black pepper

Lemon wedges, for garnish

Plain yogurt

This is a delightful variation on the stuffed-artichoke theme. If you have previously not liked couscous because it was too gummy, the problem was, you followed the directions. For perfect, fluffy couscous, never cook it. Just pour boiling liquid over it. This versatile dish can be served warm or cold.

Trim, cook, and drain the artichokes (page 11), and set aside. Bring the chicken broth to a boil. Put the couscous in a bowl and pour the boiling chicken broth over it, cover and set aside for about 30 minutes. Heat the olive oil in a heavy skillet and gently sauté the onion and garlic until the onion is pinkish but not yet beginning to brown. Add the tomato, curry, dill weed, and cumin, and continue to sauté for another minute or two. Using a table fork, fluff the couscous and add the tomato-and-onion mixture. Add the currants, pine nuts or almonds, sugar, green onion, and lemon juice and zest. Fluff gently. Add the additional olive oil and season to taste with salt and pepper. Fluff again and set aside.

Carefully spread the leaves of each artichoke apart and remove the choke (page 13). Gently pack some of the couscous mixture into the center of each artichoke and among some of the leaves. Place the stuffed artichokes on individual serving plates. Garnish with wedges of lemon and accompany with a bowl of plain yogurt.

Tuscan-style Stuffed Artichokes
xxxxxx

Bread crumbs and herbs combine to make this special-occasion dish. I prefer to use Italian or French bread for the crumbs.

Preheat oven to 350 degrees F. Trim and cook the artichokes, along with the stems (page 11). Drain well, and finely chop the stems. Heat the olive oil in a heavy skillet, and gently sauté the onion and garlic until the onion is pinkish and translucent but not yet beginning to brown. Add the diced tomato, basil, Italian seasoning, and chopped artichoke stems, and sauté for about a minute. Set aside and allow to cool. Toss the bread crumbs, cheeses, green onions, and parsley together. Add the cooled onion-and-tomato mixture and mix gently. Season to taste with salt and pepper.

Carefully spread the leaves of the artichokes apart and remove the chokes (page 13). Gently pack the filling into the center of the artichokes and between some of the leaves. Place the stuffed artichokes in a baking dish in the center of the oven just until the cheeses are melted and beginning to bubble and brown. Remove from the oven and allow to cool a bit before serving.

Makes 2

2 large artichokes

1–2 tablespoons olive oil

1 medium-size yellow onion, diced

4–6 cloves garlic, minced

1 large ripe tomato, seeded and diced

2 tablespoons chopped fresh basil leaves

1 teaspoon Italian seasoning

2 cups bread crumbs

½ cup grated mozzarella

½ cup grated fresh Parmesan

2 green onions, chopped small

About 1 tablespoon chopped parsley

Salt and freshly coarse-ground black pepper

Baby Artichoke Frittata

xxxxxx

Serves 3–4

4 eggs

¼ cup cream

Salt and freshly coarse-ground black pepper

1–2 tablespoons olive oil

1 medium-size yellow onion, chopped

4–6 cloves garlic, minced

½ ripe red bell pepper, seeded and diced

½ teaspoon Italian seasoning

8–10 canned water-pack artichoke hearts or baby artichokes, well drained and sliced

⅓ cup grated mozzarella

⅓ cup grated sharp Cheddar

⅓ cup grated fresh Parmesan

About 2 tablespoons finely chopped fresh basil leaves

2–3 tablespoons sliced olives

1 teaspoon capers

Olive oil

Sprigs of fresh basil, for garnish

This Italian variation on the omelet theme always hits the spot, and never more than when given a California twist.

Preheat oven to 350 degrees F. Beat the eggs and cream together with a bit of salt and pepper. Heat the oil in a heavy skillet with an ovenproof handle, and gently sauté the onion and garlic until the onion is pinkish and translucent. Add the bell pepper and Italian seasoning, and continue to sauté until the pepper is hot through and the onions are just beginning to brown. Add the sliced artichoke hearts. Slowly pour the beaten eggs into the pan. Scatter about two-thirds of the cheeses evenly over the top, and with the back of a fork gently agitate the surface to incorporate the cheeses into the uncooked egg, being careful not to disturb the bottom. Scatter the basil, olives, and capers over all and allow to cook for about a minute. Scatter the remaining cheeses over the top and put the skillet in the center of the preheated oven. Bake for about 15 minutes or until the egg is set and the cheeses are melted and just beginning to brown. Remove from the oven and drizzle with a bit of olive oil. Allow to sit for a minute or two before sliding onto a serving plate. Garnish with sprigs of fresh basil. If you are a confirmed carnivore you could add crumbled bacon, slivered ham, or diced grilled chicken breast to this dish.

Artichoke Hearts, Roasted Peppers, and Prosciutto on Fettuccine

xxxxxx

Serves 4–6

5–6 ounces dry fettuccine

A few drops olive oil

2 tablespoons additional olive oil

1 yellow onion, diced

4–6 cloves fresh garlic, chopped

1 can (14½-ounces) water-pack artichoke hearts

1 roasted pepper (page 84), seeded and cut into julienne

½ cup pitted black olives, crushed

½ cup pitted Kalamata olives

8–10 cloves roasted garlic (page 83), coarsely chopped

1 large ripe tomato, diced

¼ cup chopped fresh basil leaves

½ cup slivered prosciutto

½ cup chicken broth

¼ cup red wine

Dried chile flakes

Salt and freshly coarse-ground black pepper

Curls of fresh Parmesan

Chopped parsley

Here is another sunny Mediterranean dish—delicious, simple, and not too hard on the waistline.

Bring a large pot of water to boil and cook the fettuccine to your desired degree of doneness. Drain but do not rinse. Add a bit of olive oil, toss gently, cover, and set aside.

Heat the 2 tablespoons of olive oil in a heavy skillet and gently sauté the onion and fresh garlic until the onion is just beginning to brown around the edges. Depending on the size, halve or quarter the artichoke hearts and add to the skillet. Add the roasted pepper, olives, roasted garlic, tomato, basil, prosciutto, chicken broth, wine, and chile flakes, and simmer for about 5 minutes. Season to taste with salt and pepper. Add the fettuccine to the skillet, toss gently to heat through, and remove to a serving plate. Scatter the top generously with curls of fresh Parmesan and a bit of parsley.

Baby Artichokes and Chicken Breast Sauté

xxxxxx

Light, luscious, and easy, this dish is just the ticket when there is little time but the occasion calls for something special.

Bring a large pot of water to a boil and add the pasta. Cook to desired degree of doneness. Drain but do not rinse. Add a few drops of olive oil, cover, and set aside. Drain the artichokes and set aside. Heat the 2 tablespoons of olive oil in a heavy skillet and brown the chicken on all sides. Remove from the pan and keep warm. Add the onion and garlic to the skillet and sauté until the onion is soft and just beginning to brown around the edges. Deglaze the pan with the Sherry. Add the artichokes and Italian seasoning and sauté until the artichokes are hot through. Return the chicken to the pan and stir in the mustard, coating everything evenly. Add the chicken broth and basil, stir gently, and simmer for a minute or 2. Add the pasta, stir gently, and season to taste with salt and pepper. Cook only until the pasta is reheated. Remove to a serving plate and sprinkle with the Parmesan and parsley.

Serves 4–6

1 pound radiatori, quadrefiore, orecchiette, or medium shells

A few drops of olive oil

1 can (14½ ounces) water-pack artichoke hearts

About 2 tablespoons additional olive oil

2–3 boneless, skinned chicken breasts cut into bite-size chunks

1 yellow onion, cut into slices and each slice quartered

4–6 cloves garlic, chopped

¼ cup inexpensive cream Sherry

1 teaspoon Italian seasoning

1 tablespoon sweet and hot brown mustard (page 86)

½ cup chicken broth

About ¼ cup chopped fresh basil leaves

Salt and freshly coarse-ground black pepper

½ cup grated fresh Parmesan

¼ cup chopped fresh parsley

Pasta in Artichoke Bowl

XXXXXX

For this fun dish you will need to find pastina, which is any of several varieties of very small pasta such as orzo, stelle, occhi, or anellini. This dish makes a perfect romantic dinner two people can share.

Trim, cook, and drain the artichoke (page 11), and allow to cool. Remove the choke (page 13). Set aside. Put the pasta into a pot of boiling water and cook to desired degree of doneness. Drain but do not rinse. Add a few drops of olive oil, cover, and set aside.

Preheat oven to 350 degrees F. Heat the 2 tablespoons of olive oil in a heavy skillet and gently sauté the onion, garlic, celery, and pepper together until all are soft and just beginning to brown around the edges. Add the tomato, tomato paste, wine, and Italian seasoning, and stir gently until the tomato paste is evenly distributed. Drain the clams and measure the liquid. Add enough chicken broth to make 1½ cups liquid total. Add to the skillet and adjust the heat to maintain a rapid simmer. Continue to cook, stirring occasionally until the liquid is almost evaporated but the ingredients are not dry. Add the olives, clams, parsley, and cooked pasta, and cook for another minute or 2. Remove from heat and allow to cool. When the mixture is cooled, gently fold in the cheeses and season to taste with salt and pepper. Set the artichoke on a heatproof serving plate and gently spread the leaves apart to increase the size of the opening in the center. Pile the pasta mixture into the center and place in the oven for about 5 minutes or until the cheeses begin to melt and slightly brown around the edges.

Serves 2

1 large artichoke

About 2 ounces cooked pastina

A few drops olive oil

About 2 tablespoons additional olive oil

1 medium-size yellow onion, diced

4–6 cloves garlic, minced

About ½ cup finely chopped celery

About ½ bell pepper, seeded and diced

1 large ripe tomato, chopped

2 tablespoons tomato paste

¼ cup red wine

½ teaspoon Italian seasoning

1 can chopped or minced clams

Chicken broth

¼ cup chopped black olives

¼ cup finely chopped fresh parsley

About ½ cup grated mozzarella

About ¼ cup grated Parmesan

Salt and freshly coarse-ground black pepper

Artichoke Quiche

xxxxx

Makes one 8–9-inch quiche

1 pie shell, 8–9 inches (your favorite recipe or page 82)

1 egg white beaten with 1 tablespoon cold water

1–2 tablespoons olive oil

1 medium-size yellow onion, diced

3–4 cloves garlic, minced

1 can (14 ounces) artichoke hearts, drained and sliced thinly

3 eggs plus 1 egg yolk, lightly beaten

1½ cups half-and-half

¼ teaspoon ground nutmeg

¼ teaspoon dry dill weed

About ⅔ cup cooked baby shrimp meat, chopped

⅓ cup grated mozzarella

⅓ cup grated extra-sharp Cheddar

¼ cup chopped fresh parsley

Salt and freshly coarse-ground black pepper

¼ cup grated fresh Parmesan

Sour cream

Quiche is one of those dishes that people tend to be afraid to try making; it sounds daunting. However, if you can make a pumpkin pie you can make a quiche.

Preheat oven to 350 degrees F. Line an 8- to 9-inch pan with the pie shell. Paint the pastry with the egg white. Set aside.

Heat the olive oil in a heavy skillet and gently sauté the onion and garlic until the onion is soft, translucent, and just beginning to brown around the edges. Add the sliced artichokes and continue to sauté until the artichoke begins to brown. Remove from heat and allow to cool.

Bring a kettle of water to boil. Meanwhile, whisk the eggs and half-and-half together with the nutmeg and dill weed. When cool, sprinkle the onion-and-artichoke mixture on the bottom of the prepared pastry shell, then add the shrimp meat. Toss the mozzarella and Cheddar together with the parsley and scatter over the top of the shrimp. Season to taste with salt and pepper. Place the pie plate inside a larger baking dish and set on the center rack of the preheated oven. Working quickly, pour the egg-and-cream mixture into the pie shell until it is full. Scatter the Parmesan over the top. Add enough of the boiling water to the larger baking pan to come halfway up the sides of the pie dish. Bake for about 40 minutes or until a bamboo skewer inserted into the center comes out clean. Remove from the oven and allow to sit until room temperature before slicing. Top each serving with a dollop of sour cream.

Artichokes Gratinées
xxxxxx

This is another delicious, yet simple dish that takes advantage of frozen or canned water-pack baby artichokes or artichoke hearts.

Preheat oven to 350 degrees F. Drain artichokes and set aside. Heat the oil in a heavy skillet and gently sauté the onion, garlic and fennel root until the onion is translucent and pinkish and just beginning to brown around the edges. Remove from the pan and set aside. When as much moisture as possible has drained from the artichokes, slice them. Add a bit more oil to the skillet if necessary and sauté the artichokes until just beginning to brown. Set aside with the onion mixture. Add a bit more oil to the skillet and sauté the mushrooms until they are hot through, only about a minute or 2. Set aside. Toss the basil, cheeses, bread crumbs, Italian seasoning, and salt and pepper (to taste) together in a bowl.

Arrange half the onion, garlic, and fennel mixture in the bottom of a casserole dish. Scatter half the artichokes and half the mushrooms over the mixture, and top with half the slices of tomato. Scatter half the cheese and bread crumb mixture over all. Repeat the entire process in a second layer. When all is ready, place in the preheated oven for 25 to 30 minutes or until the cheeses are melted and just beginning to turn brown. Serve hot.

Serves 4–6

1 can (14 ounces) water-pack baby artichokes or frozen equivalent

1–2 tablespoons olive oil

1 large yellow onion, cut into ¼-inch thick rings, the rings quartered

6–8 cloves garlic, chopped

About ½ cup thinly slivered fresh fennel root

1 cup sliced mushrooms

¼ cup chopped fresh basil leaves

⅓ cup grated fresh mozzarella

⅓ cup grated sharp Cheddar

⅓ cup grated Parmesan

½ cup dry bread crumbs (French or Italian style)

A pinch of Italian seasoning

Salt and freshly coarse-ground black pepper

2–3 ripe tomatoes, sliced

Easy Grilled Artichokes

xxxxxx

Makes 8 servings of half an artichoke each

4 large artichokes

¼ cup balsamic vinegar

¼ cup olive oil

¼ cup soy sauce

1 tablespoon sweet and hot brown mustard (page 86)

1 teaspoon Worcestershire sauce

½ teaspoon sesame oil

This easy recipe is made even easier because you can do all the prep work the day before.

Trim, cook, and drain the artichokes (page 11). When artichokes are cool enough to handle, slice in half lengthwise and remove the choke (page 13). Put all remaining ingredients into a large plastic bag and mix well. Add the artichoke halves, seal the bag, and refrigerate overnight. Gently agitate the bag occasionally to insure even marinating.

Drain well and reserve the marinade. Place the artichokes cut-side-down over a bed of coals and cook for 5 or 6 minutes, or until the tips of the leaves just begin to char. Turn the artichokes and grill for another 3 or 4 minutes on the other side. Serve warm or at room temperature with a bit of the marinade for dipping.

Artichoke Risotto

xxxxx

Serves 4–6

4–5 cups chicken broth

2 tablespoons olive oil

1 large yellow onion, diced

4–6 cloves garlic, minced

1 cup Arborio rice

½ cup white wine

1 jar (6 ounces) marinated
artichoke hearts, drained
and chopped

¼ cup pine nuts or
slivered almonds

½ cup grated fresh
Parmesan

¼ cup crumbled
Gorgonzola cheese

¼ cup chopped
fresh parsley

Salt and freshly coarse-
ground black pepper

I am told that I make very good risotto despite the fact that I can't stand it. I grew up in the Oriental and Latino rice traditions. To me, rice should always be fluffy. I have nothing against the flavor of risotto; it's the texture I don't like. However, I think the risotto fans among you will be very pleased with this recipe.

Heat the chicken broth and keep it just below a simmer. Heat the olive oil in the bottom of a large heavy pot and gently sauté the onion and garlic until they are just beginning to brown. Add the rice and, stirring all the while, cook over a moderate heat until all is evenly coated with the oil. Add the wine and continue to cook, stirring until the wine has been absorbed. Now begin adding the hot chicken broth, ½ cup at a time, and cooking while gently stirring after each addition. Continue in this manner until the rice is tender and creamy. Add the chopped artichoke hearts and the pine nuts or almonds. Continue cooking and stirring until all the liquid has been absorbed by the rice.

Turn off the heat and add the cheeses and parsley. Stir gently. Season to taste with salt and pepper.

Artichoke, Crab, and Provolone Rolls

xxxxxx

Sandwiches don't have to be relegated to the lunchbox. Try this elegant and satisfying variation on the sandwich theme. The Earl of Sandwich himself would find this a worthy meal.

Split the French rolls in half and remove about half of the crumb from the bottom half of each. Chop the artichoke hearts and place in a bowl. Add the crabmeat, garlic, green onion, dill, and mustard, and mix gently. Add enough mayonnaise to make into a spreadable consistency. Season to taste with lemon juice, salt, and pepper. Fill the bottom half of each roll with this mixture. Top with slices of tomato and cheese. Put under the broiler just until the cheese begins to melt. Remove and top with the other half of the roll. Serve warm.

Makes 2

2 crusty French-type rolls

1 jar (6 ounces) marinated artichoke hearts, drained

About ½ cup crabmeat

3–4 cloves roasted garlic, finely minced (page 83)

1 green onion, finely chopped, including most of the green

Pinch of dry dill weed or 1 teaspoon finely chopped fresh

1 teaspoon sweet and hot brown mustard (page 86)

About ½ cup mayonnaise

Lemon juice

Salt and freshly coarse-ground black pepper

1 large ripe tomato, sliced

2–3 slices of provolone cheese

Chicken Breasts with Artichokes and Mushrooms

xxxxxx

Serves 4

2 skinless, boneless chicken breasts

Salt and freshly coarse-ground black pepper

1 teaspoon paprika

1 tablespoon taco seasoning

1–2 tablespoons olive oil

1 medium-size yellow onion, diced

½ pound small mushrooms, sliced

1 jar (6 ounces) marinated artichoke hearts, drained, marinade reserved

2–3 green onions, chopped, including the greens

½ cup white wine

½ cup chicken broth

Chicken, mushrooms, and artichoke hearts form a perfect union in this lightly Latino dish.

Preheat oven to 350 degrees F. Cut the chicken breasts in half and rub on all sides with salt and pepper. Mix the paprika and taco seasoning together, and rub this onto the chicken as well. Heat the oil in a heavy skillet, and gently sauté the chicken until golden-brown on all sides. Arrange the chicken in a baking dish. Gently sauté the yellow onions until they are just beginning to brown. Scatter them over the chicken. Sauté the mushrooms and scatter over the chicken as well. Slice the artichokes in half and arrange over the chicken along with the green onions. Mix the marinade, wine, and chicken broth together and pour over the ingredients in the baking dish. Bake in the center of the oven until the chicken is cooked to desired degree of doneness, about 35 to 40 minutes. Test for doneness by slicing into the thickest part of a piece of chicken. It should be opaque, not translucent. Serve with steamed rice.

Artichoke Shrimp Fajitas

xxxxxx

Talk about fusion cuisine! Here is a very definite California take on the fajita theme. And it's so easy. If shrimp isn't your fancy, you could substitute strips of grilled chicken breast.

Heat the olive oil in a heavy skillet and gently sauté the onions, garlic, and bell pepper until soft and the onions are just beginning to brown. Drain the artichokes and cut into quarters. Add to the skillet along with the shrimp, salsa, and cilantro, and continue to cook over a moderate heat only until all is hot through. Add salt and pepper to taste. Serve with warm flour tortillas.

Serves 4–6

1–2 tablespoons olive oil

1 medium-size yellow onion, sliced into thin rings

4–6 cloves garlic, minced

1 ripe, red bell pepper, seeded and cut into thin julienne

2 jars (6 ounces each) marinated artichoke hearts

½ pound cooked baby shrimp meat

1 cup of your favorite salsa, mighty or mild

¼ cup chopped fresh cilantro

Salt and freshly coarse-ground black pepper

Flour tortillas

Artichokes Normandy

xxxxxx

Serves 4

4 large artichokes

6 tablespoons butter

6 tablespoons
all-purpose flour

2 cups heavy cream

1 cup white wine

1 cup grated mozzarella

½ cup grated
sharp Cheddar

½ teaspoon ground nutmeg

Salt and black pepper

2 additional
tablespoons butter

½ pound sliced mushrooms

Fresh grated Parmesan

Paprika

Here is a delectable dish that takes your taste buds one step beyond. Damn the calories! Full speed ahead!

Trim, cook, and drain the artichokes (page 11). Remove the chokes (page 13). Place in a baking dish. Preheat the oven to 350 degrees F. In a heavy saucepan melt the 6 tablespoons of butter and flour together, stirring until well blended. When it begins to foam, slowly whisk in the cream. Continue whisking for 2 or 3 minutes, then slowly whisk in the wine, and continue to whisk until the mixture returns to the consistency of thick cream. Gently stir in the cheeses and stir until the cheeses have melted. Add the nutmeg, and season to taste with salt and pepper. Set aside.

In a heavy skillet, melt the 2 tablespoons of butter and gently sauté the mushrooms until they are hot through, translucent, and just beginning to brown around the edges. Divide the mushrooms between the 4 artichokes, placing them in the cavity in the center. Pour the wine sauce into and over the artichokes. Top with a sprinkling of Parmesan and paprika and bake in the center of the oven for about 20 minutes. Serve hot.

Andalusian Fish Fillets with Artichokes and Olives

xxxxxx

The very essence of the Mediterranean, this delicious dish will bring sunshine to any table.

Serves 4

Preheat oven to 350 degrees F. Heat the olive oil in a heavy skillet and gently sauté the onion and garlic until the onion is just beginning to brown around the edges. Add the canned and fresh tomatoes, rosemary, and wine, and bring to the boil, then reduce the heat to a rapid simmer and continue to cook until the mixture has formed a thick sauce, about 20 minutes. Meanwhile, drain and chop the artichokes. When the sauce has thickened, add the artichokes and olives and season to taste with salt and pepper. Add the parsley and cook for another minute or two. Set aside. Place the fillets in a baking dish and pour the sauce over. Place in the center of the oven and bake about 20–30 minutes, until the flesh is opaque.

2 tablespoons olive oil

1 yellow onion, chopped

4–6 cloves garlic, chopped

1 can (14½ oz.) crushed or diced tomatoes

2 fresh tomatoes, diced

1 teaspoon finely minced fresh rosemary

¼ cup red wine

2 jars (6 ounces each) marinated artichoke hearts

1 can (2 ¼ ounces) of sliced black olives, drained

Salt and freshly coarse-ground black pepper

¼ cup chopped fresh parsley

4 boneless fillets of mild white fish (sole, snapper, butterfish, etc.)

Artichokes Étouffée

xxxxxx

Serves 4–6

Étouffée means "smothered." This Cajun-inspired dish is smothered in a robust red sauce that may be as mighty or mild as you wish.

8–10 small fresh artichokes (about 3 inches long)

1 lemon, cut in half

1–2 tablespoons olive oil

1 yellow onion, diced

6–8 cloves garlic, chopped

1 rib celery, chopped small

1 bell pepper, seeded and chopped small

1 can (15½ ounces) diced tomatoes

Italian seasoning

1 sprig fresh rosemary

1 bay leaf

Dry chile flakes

¼ cup red wine

1 tablespoon sugar

Salt and freshly coarse-ground black pepper

1 can (14½ ounces) chicken broth or about 2 cups

½ cup grated sharp Cheddar

Pull the small superficial leaves off the artichokes. Then snap off the remaining leaves. If you bend back the leaves of a fresh artichoke one at a time, they should snap off at the beginning of the meaty part. Slice each artichoke in half, remove any of the remaining small leaves that have a purple tinge to them, and scrape or cut out the chokes. Rub the cut side of each artichoke with lemon, and place cut-side-down in a casserole dish. Preheat oven to 350 degrees F.

Heat the olive oil in a heavy skillet, and, over moderate heat, sauté the onions and garlic until the onions are soft, translucent, and just beginning to brown around the edges. Add the celery and bell pepper and continue to sauté until all are well coated with oil and beginning to soften, 2 to 3 minutes more. Add the tomatoes, Italian seasoning, rosemary, bay leaf, chile flakes, wine, and sugar. Bring to a boil and then reduce heat to maintain a rapid simmer. Continue to cook for about 10 minutes or until thickened. Season to taste with salt and pepper. Pour over the artichokes in the casserole. Add the chicken broth, cover with aluminum foil, and place in the center of the oven. Bake for about 45 minutes or until the artichokes are tender. Remove the foil. If there appears to be too much liquid remaining, bake uncovered for 5 to 10 minutes or until most of the liquid is absorbed. Sprinkle with the cheese and bake just until the cheese begins to melt. Serve hot with fluffy rice.

Pilaf-Stuffed Artichokes

xxxxxx

Here is yet another variation on the stuffed-artichoke theme.

Makes 4

Heat the olive oil in a heavy skillet, and gently sauté the onion and garlic until the onion is translucent and pinkish but not yet beginning to brown. Add the Italian seasoning, dill weed, nutmeg, cumin, pine nuts, and currants and continue to cook, stirring gently until all ingredients are coated with the oil. Add the rice, and stir over medium heat until evenly mixed. Pour in the 2 cups of chicken broth and bring to the boil. Continue to boil until the level of the liquid has evaporated to the level of the rice. Cover with a tight-fitting lid and set aside to steam for about 20 minutes or to al dente stage. Remove the lid, add the green onions and parsley, and fluff the rice. Season to taste with salt and pepper.

Preheat the oven to 350 degrees F. While the rice is steaming, evenly trim the bottoms of the artichokes, spread the leaves, and remove the chokes. With a pair of kitchen shears, snip off the sticker at the end of each artichoke leaf. Spread the leaves of the artichokes out to enlarge the hollow in the center, and pack the rice mixture into them. Set the artichokes upright in a deep casserole with a tight-fitting lid and pour in enough chicken broth to come about ⅔ of the way up the artichokes. Cover with the lid and place in the center of the oven. Bake for 40 to 45 minutes or until a leaf may be removed easily. When the artichokes are done, remove them to a serving dish and place the casserole dish on top of the stove, and boil gently until the liquid is reduced by half. Add the butter and Sherry and simmer until the butter is melted. Strain and pour over the artichokes on the serving dish.

1–2 tablespoons olive oil

1 medium yellow onion, chopped

4–6 garlic cloves, minced

½ teaspoon Italian seasoning

1 tablespoon minced fresh dill weed

¼ teaspoon ground nutmeg

¼ teaspoon ground cumin

¼ cup pine nuts

¼ cup currants

1 cup long-grain white rice

2 cups chicken broth

2 green onions, chopped small, including most of the green

¼ cup chopped parsley

Salt and freshly coarse-ground black pepper

4 large artichokes

Additional chicken broth for cooking

2 tablespoons butter

¼ cup inexpensive cream Sherry

Braised Chicken and Artichokes Athenian

xxxxxx

Serves 4

1–2 tablespoons olive oil

1 yellow onion, diced

6–8 cloves garlic, chopped

2 boneless and skinless chicken breasts

Salt and freshly coarse-ground black pepper

¼ cup red wine

⅔ cup chicken broth

1 tablespoon fresh lemon juice

1 teaspoon lemon zest

1 tablespoon sugar

Dry crushed chiles

1 tablespoon chopped fresh Mediterranean oregano (not Mexican)

2 jars (6 ounces each) marinated artichoke hearts, drained, marinade reserved

½ cup pitted Greek olives

2 lemons, cut into wedges

This Greek-inspired dish is a perfect vehicle for marinated artichoke hearts. To carry out the Greek theme you might use it in a meal that begins with dolmas (stuffed grape leaves). Sophocles himself would be comfortable at your table.

Heat the olive oil in a heavy skillet, and gently sauté the onion and garlic until the onion is just beginning to brown around the edges. Remove from the skillet and set aside. Cut the chicken breasts in half, and rub each piece with salt and pepper. Sauté in the skillet until well browned on all sides. Remove from the pan and set aside. Deglaze the pan with the wine and return the onions to the pan. Add the broth, lemon juice, zest, sugar, dried chiles to taste, and oregano. Stir well and bring to a boil. Reduce heat to a simmer and return the chicken to the pan. Add the artichoke hearts, olives, and lemon wedges. Cover with a tight-fitting lid and cook for an additional 15–20 minutes or until the chicken is cooked through. Serve with rice.

These recipes can be used with other dishes in this cookbook. They are all handy items to have in your pantry or refrigerator.

Perfect Pastry

xxxxxx

Makes enough for 2 double-crust 8–9-inch pies

5 cups all-purpose flour

1 pound cold butter, margarine, shortening, or lard, or combination thereof

1 tablespoon distilled white vinegar

1 raw egg

Cold water

This is the finest pastry recipe I have ever used. I use it for all my pastry needs, sweet and savory. The recipe makes enough for 2 double-crust 8–9-inch pies, but don't worry. If you don't use it all, divide it, form into disks that are about ½-inch thick, wrap well, label, and freeze. Warning: allow to thaw at room temperature. Do not try to thaw in the microwave.

Put the flour into a large bowl. Cut the butter into small pieces and toss with the flour. With a wire pastry blender, work the butter into the flour until it is the texture of coarse cornmeal. Do not use a food processor. Put the vinegar and egg in a liquid measuring cup and mix well. Add enough cold water to bring the total amount of liquid to 1 cup. Stir and add to the flour-and-butter mixture. With a table fork, stir round and round until the liquid has moistened all the dry ingredients and they have been gathered into a ball. Turn out onto a lightly floured surface and knead gently, actually just pushing it together. Divide the dough into 2 portions and flatten each into a disk about ½-inch thick. Wrap in plastic and chill well before using. This dough freezes well, and I like to always have some on hand.

Roasted Garlic

xxxxxx

Cloves of roasted garlic are wonderful helpmates to have hanging around your kitchen. If you had to make them fresh for every recipe you would never bother; however, if you keep some on hand you will find a myriad of uses for them.

Makes about ½ pound

½ teaspoon olive oil

1 jar (8 ounces) peeled garlic cloves *

Wipe a heavy skillet with the oil. Add all of the garlic, making sure that the cloves are only one layer deep. Cook the garlic over a medium heat until it just begins to turn golden on the bottom side. Flip the cloves over and continue to cook until that side is just beginning to show color. Shake the pan frequently while cooking. Continue in this manner, shaking the pan and flipping the garlic, until the cloves have become a golden brown and are somewhat soft. The entire process will take about 30 minutes. Do it on a day when you are going to be in the kitchen anyway. When done, allow to cool and then put in a jar and store in the refrigerator.

*Christopher Ranch is one of the largest manufacturers of this product. Visit www.christopherranch.com. If you can't find them ready-peeled, you can of course peel your own.

Roasted Peppers

XXXXXX

Makes as many as you want

Bell peppers or chiles

Tongs

Old clean tea towel or other clean cloth or brown paper bag

Roasted peppers are also handy to have on hand. They are available commercially, but they are quite expensive and usually come in very small amounts. I make these whenever I find red bell peppers on sale. You may use this same technique for roasting hot or mild chiles for salsas and other dishes. Some people think these require a gas range, but I made them on an electric stove for years before I was finally able to install a gas range.

When choosing your peppers or chiles, choose ones that have the fewest convolutions to the surface. If they have many valleys and peaks it is difficult to evenly blister the skin.

Some people like to roast their peppers in the oven. I do not. That method cooks the pepper in addition to blackening the skin, and I don't want my peppers cooked. I just want to char the skin.

If you have a gas range, place a wire rack over the burner. If you have electric you will work directly on the burner. Of course, the very best way to roast peppers and chiles is in the back yard over your grill or barbecue.

Do not cut or seed the peppers before you roast them. Lay your peppers or chiles on the wire rack or burner and allow to sit until the skin begins to blacken and blister. Use the tongs to turn the pepper to a new spot and allow it to blacken as well. Continue in this manner, turning the peppers as they blacken, until most of the surface has been blistered. Remove from the heat and wrap in the cloth or place in the paper bag. This allows the pepper to steam a bit and makes the skin easier to remove.

Do only 2–3 peppers at a time, because you want them to sit for a few minutes so the steam will help loosen the skin. Peel them before they cool down, or it will become very difficult to get the skin off.

Let the peppers sit in the cloth or bag for about 3–5 minutes, then take them to the sink and gently rub the surface under cold running water to remove the charred skin. Any skin that is a bit stubborn may be scraped off with your thumbnail or a small paring knife. Once you have removed as much of the charred skin as possible, you may trim and seed the peppers. Your roasted peppers are ready to toss into salads, stir-fries, and pasta dishes, or you may jar them with marinade for later use. Commercial Italian dressing plus garlic to taste makes an easy marinade.

Aioli, the Real Thing

xxxxxx

I have listed a quick and easy version of aioli using commercial mayonnaise on page 18; however, if you have the time, nothing beats the real thing.

Makes about 2 cups

2 egg yolks

4–6 cloves garlic, minced

1 teaspoon dry powdered mustard

1 teaspoon lemon juice

Salt

Sugar

Finely minced fresh tarragon or dill weed

¼ cup fresh white bread crumbs

2 cups extra virgin olive oil

If you have a large mortar and pestle, that is the best thing to use. Put the egg yolks, garlic, mustard, lemon juice, salt, and sugar to taste, herbs, and bread crumbs in the bottom of the mortar and using the pestle, you begin pounding and mixing until you have a very smooth paste, then begin slowly adding the oil while still pounding and mixing.

If you don't have a mortar and pestle, put all ingredients except the oil in a bowl and blend into submission with a handheld electric rotary mixer. When the mixture is smooth and thickened, begin adding the oil in the same manner you do when making mayonnaise (page 87). Aioli is a superb enhancement for many dishes.

Sweet and Hot Brown Mustard
XXXXXX

Makes about 2 cups

½ cup brown mustard seeds

½ cup yellow mustard seeds

1 cup yellow mustard powder

1 cup sugar

Cider vinegar

This excellent mustard is not only a great condiment (try it on a kielbasa sandwich), it is also an essential ingredient in many dishes. If you try to buy enough mustard powder at regular grocery-store prices you will have to refinance your house. Go to a supplier that sells herbs and spices in bulk, or visit www.sfherb.com, where you can buy it for a fraction of the price.

Put the mustard seeds in the jar of a blender and pulse. You do not want to turn them into powder. You just want to crack them. The proper texture will be a mixture: Most of them will be cracked, some will remain whole, and some will become powder. Remove to a large bowl. Add the mustard powder and sugar and stir well. Begin pouring in the vinegar, stirring as you do. Continue to stir in vinegar until you reach the proper consistency. The consistency should be that of thick cream.

Be warned. The first day you make this mustard the taste will be rather harsh and somewhat unpleasant. After it sits for several days the flavor mellows and becomes wonderful. There is no need to refrigerate this mustard. I have kept it on my pantry shelf for months. As it sits it may thicken, but if it becomes too thick, just stir in more cider vinegar until it reaches the proper consistency again.

Mayonnaise

xxxxxx

Good mayonnaise is not difficult to make; it just takes patience. It is absolutely essential that the oil be added VERY slowly.

Put egg yolks into a bowl and add the lemon juice, salt, sugar, and mustard powder. With an electric rotary beater, blend for about a minute or until the mixture is well blended, creamy, smooth, golden, and somewhat thickened. Now—and this is the really important part—begin adding the oil, 1 tablespoon at a time only, beating it in well after each addition. Continue in this manner until the mixture has emulsified (thickened). At this point you may begin adding the oil a bit faster. When all the oil has been added you should have a lovely, tight, creamy mayonnaise. Taste and adjust seasonings, adding more lemon, salt, sugar, or mustard as desired.

And YES! It uses a raw egg! There is only one chance in 20,000 that you will get a contaminated egg. Your chances of being killed in a car are much higher than your risk of getting sick from eating a raw egg.

*You may use 1 whole egg instead of 2 egg yolks. If you are trying to cut your cholesterol you may also use 2 egg whites instead of the yolks. Neither variation will produce a product that is as thick as the egg yolk version.

Makes about 2 cups

2 egg yolks *

1 teaspoon lemon juice

½ teaspoon salt

½ teaspoon sugar

1 teaspoon dry yellow mustard powder

2 cups vegetable oil